THE A TO Z OF
MODERN
MANNERS

ALSO BY DAVID MEAGHER

It's Not Etiquette

Fashion Speak

THE A TO Z OF
MODERN
MANNERS

DAVID MEAGHER

A Guide to Behaving Well

VINTAGE BOOKS
Australia

A Vintage book
Published by Penguin Random House Australia Pty Ltd
Level 3, 100 Pacific Highway, North Sydney NSW 2060
www.penguin.com.au

First published by Vintage in 2016

Addresses for the Penguin Random House group of companies can be found
at global.penguinrandomhouse.com/offices.

National Library of Australia
Cataloguing-in-Publication entry

Meagher, David, 1966– author
The A to Z of modern manners: a guide to behaving well/David Meagher

ISBN 978 0 85798 367 1 (paperback)

Online social networks
Etiquette
Business etiquette

302.30285

Cover design by Natalie Winter
Typeset in 11.5/16 pt Sabon by Midland Typesetters, Australia
Printed in Australia by Griffin Press, an accredited ISO AS/NZS 14001:2004
Environmental Management System printer

Penguin Random House Australia uses papers that are natural, renewable
and recyclable products and made from wood grown in sustainable forests.
The logging and manufacturing processes are expected to conform to the
environmental regulations of the country of origin.

CONTENTS

INTRODUCTION

There have been many moments when I thought I wouldn't write this book.

Time was one of the main reasons. Like many writers, I have a day job. I started this book and abandoned it on more occasions than I or my publisher would care to be reminded of. Clearly I changed my mind, though, or you wouldn't be reading this now. I realise we're only on the second paragraph so, before I lose you, let me explain a little more about why I didn't want to write this book and the reasons for my change of heart – it might help answer the question, does the world really need another book on manners?

I didn't want to write this book because I didn't want to be that person who tells others how to behave. It's very hard to write a book on manners without focusing on perceived instances of bad behaviour, and that means you need to start a lot of sentences with the word 'don't'. This book should help people do the right thing and I hope I have managed to accentuate the positive along the way without concentrating too much on the negative.

I know, because I've been that person before. This is not my first book on the subject of manners. In 2005 I wrote a book called *It's Not Etiquette: A guide to modern manners*, and it was a mild success. Not that you will find it on the shelves of your local bookshop now. That's just the reality of book publishing. Unless you write a blockbuster, when your book is sold out, that's it.

Don't feel bad for me, though – I'm not complaining about the situation. Far from it, in fact. While I am just as driven by pride and money as the next person, when that book had reached the end of its shelf life I was well and truly ready to move on.

It's Not Etiquette was a guide to manners with a particular emphasis on the workplace and the growing use of technology in our lives. It sounds kind of quaint to say that now but it was 2005 and, as hard as it might be to believe, technology was really only just beginning to transform our everyday lives. My concept for the book was that it would look at historical texts on etiquette and manners and apply them to contemporary life, which was changing at a rapid pace thanks to the rise of the digital. *It's Not Etiquette* was meant to be informative and authoritative but it was also meant to be lighthearted. That's why I called it *It's Not Etiquette*. I didn't want people to think it was a boring book by some pompous know-it-all – who would want to read that? Etiquette is a word from a bygone era and the very thought of it turns people off. I figured the best way to tell people my book wasn't about the dirty word etiquette was to say it in the title.

The book got plenty of media attention and I lapped it up (book publishing was new to me), and I went on every TV and radio show I was invited onto. Even after the book was no longer available in stores I was invited to be a talking head by radio stations whenever they had a story that might, for example, involve a display of bad manners by someone in the public sphere. 'Sure, I'd be happy to,' I'd say. I never listened to any of the interviews after they had taken place, but I did once download the podcast of a particularly long one and store it in my iTunes library for posterity.

Then one day, when I was on a road trip up the coast and had my iTunes library on shuffle to pass the time, this particular podcast started to play. I was alone in my car and thought 'This might be fun to listen to,' so I let it continue. I was shocked at how much I sounded like a complete and utter twat. 'You shouldn't do this . . . never do that . . . the correct way to do that is . . .' It was like an out-of-body experience. I had a feeling I'm sure anyone who listens to talkback radio has from time to time – I wanted to yell at the people on the radio even though I knew they couldn't hear me. Only in this instance the person on the radio could hear me, because the person was me, and I sounded just awful.

Being someone who was announced by the radio show host as 'an expert on good manners and correct behaviour' made me sound like I was the fun police, so I decided to distance myself from it. I didn't want to be the go-to person for manners commentary anymore and, as luck would have it, new books were being published on the topic and I didn't need to be. I didn't return calls from radio producers, and when they did manage to get hold of me, I would make up some excuse about being too busy. Soon enough the interest in me as an authority on manners dried up. Normal life resumed.

In hindsight I probably should have seen it coming. If you want to lose friends, or at the very least get fewer invitations to dinner, write a book on manners. Not long after *It's Not Etiquette* was published I was on my way to dinner at someone's house and I got a text from the host apologising in advance for the unironed tablecloth I was about to witness, so I wouldn't be shocked when I saw it or, worse, write about it later. And people who live in glass houses shouldn't write books on manners: you will be held to a far higher standard than others, and it gets very tiring. 'David, I would have thought someone who wrote a book on manners would know better than to not let someone merge in front of you in traffic.' Better yet were the people who didn't know me when *It's Not Etiquette* was published. 'Really, you wrote a book on manners?' they would say when they found out.

So why have I changed my mind and decided to write another book on the subject? Because I'm mad as hell, and I'm not going to take it anymore. While I might have shied away from being hailed as an expert in the past, I have always been interested in manners, and I abhor crude and crass behaviour in others. But if it's true that every man becomes the thing he hates then I have become, around the edges at least, a person with bad manners.

It's not my fault, though. People have forced me to be like this. I find myself getting so irritated and annoyed by people who do things like stare straight ahead and refuse to let me into a queue of traffic that I do the same thing. I've adopted the 'if you can't beat 'em, join 'em' approach. Who bloody cares about the correct way to hold a knife and fork when every day I encounter someone texting and driving, or texting and walking, or texting in the movies? How they eat their food in private is the least of my concern compared to the bad manners on display right in front of me. (Having said that, how you hold a knife and fork is still important, and this book does contain a short section on table manners.)

And just like Peter Finch in the movie *Network*, where the line 'I'm mad as hell and I'm not going to take it anymore' comes from, I've started yelling out of windows at complete strangers. 'Put the effing phone down! . . . Why aren't you riding on the bike path? . . . Pick up that dog poo!' It's exhausting, trying to change the world from your car window. 'Watch where you're going,' I'll say to people on the street as they step out in front of me, engrossed in their mobile phones. And I've worked out why some people become cyberbullies – they're driven to it by the inanity of what others post on social media. Admit it, how many times have you wanted to comment on someone's post with 'Really, that's something you felt you needed to share with the world?' But of course you don't; you're a well-mannered person and you need to bite your tongue.

'You're starting to sound like an old man,' my partner tells me as I complain about people who walk dogs on long retractable leads and take up the entire footpath. 'Those leads are thin and aren't easy to see, so you think the dog is walking off-lead and then you trip over an invisible wire. It's just dangerous!' My partner is right, I do sound like an old man. But if that's what it takes, then so be it – every man eventually becomes an old man and I'm just fast-tracking it. Besides, being an old man seems to give you licence to correct people.

The other day I was peacefully walking down the street when a woman on a bicycle came up behind me, rang her bell and yelled 'Watch out!' So I yelled back at her, 'No, you watch out. There is a bicycle lane just there [points to the bicycle lane about one and a half metres away from where she was riding] and that's where you should be, not on the footpath.' She told me to fuck off.

I hear that a lot these days. The other day I yelled at another driver for texting while driving. I'd been behind him for a while and he was driving so slowly that when we reached a set of traffic lights I changed lanes so I could pass him when the lights turned green. When I pulled up alongside him I could see that his head was bowed and he was looking into his lap. I figured he was using his phone, so I wound down my window, sounded my car's horn and said 'Put the phone down and drive properly.' He gave me the finger and told me to fuck off.

So instead of getting angry all the time – and at the risk of becoming known as that crazy guy who yells out his car window at people – I decided the time was right to get back into the manners business.

The world has changed a lot in the decade since I wrote *It's Not Etiquette*. Back then I spent pages discussing the finer points of table manners and no time at all on social media, as it didn't exist then. I wrote in my earlier book that it was not okay to text your boss to say you were sick and wouldn't be in. Today, I wouldn't have it any other way – I don't want people calling me in the morning to tell me they're sick. A text will do just fine, thank you.

This book, which is organised alphabetically rather than thematically, addresses some of the new forces shaping the way we live, as well as some old ones. It looks at the best way to behave in a particular situation. It's not about pointing the finger at people and calling out bad behaviour (okay, there's a bit of that but I haven't named anyone); it's about using common sense and thinking about how other people might feel in a particular situation.

One of the reasons people don't like the word etiquette is that it represents a strict set of rules that governs behaviour and dress for specific situations. Often there is no explanation given as to why a certain behaviour is correct etiquette – it just *is*. The very idea of there being a 'correct' way to behave is detestable to many people. Manners does away with the idea of perfection and replaces it with thoughtfulness. It's thinking about how someone else might feel as a result of your actions; it's good old-fashioned putting yourself in someone else's shoes and thinking about your behaviour before you act. For example, there is no right or wrong way to walk and text at the same time. There is, however, a way to do it that will cause the least inconvenience for everyone else using the footpath. You can work out what form that takes by having a little empathy for your fellow humans. That's just good manners.

A

ACTIVE WEAR

A very contemporary place to start this book. The rise of active wear (that is, sports attire) as everyday clothing has done more to destroy fashion than anything since the invention of the puffer jacket. I've probably already lost a few readers but, please, bear with me. Puffer jackets are acceptable if you are in a cold climate – you know, where it snows – which is precisely what they were designed for. No one can deny that they're warm, so it's fine to wear one with casual clothes on a cold weekend in the city, but you should mix it up with something a little dressier like a woollen coat if you want to look chic occasionally.

If you don't care about looking chic and sophist-icated then you probably won't care what I have to say about active wear. It's fine for wearing while you exercise or to and from your place of exercise (which might include a quick trip to the supermarket after the gym or a coffee with friends after a power walk), but beyond that it's just slothful to wear it out of the house. And therein lies the great paradox of active wear: it's meant to convey sportiness and athleticism but when it's worn as an everyday outfit – I'm thinking of those women who team their active wear with an It bag, statement sunglasses and perfectly coiffed hair – it suggests that you're too lazy to put an outfit together in the morning. 'I'll just wear tights because it's comfortable,' you might think, but since when did comfort become the only consideration when choosing an outfit to be worn out in public? The same applies to men who wear sporting or exercise gear all day long without any intention of stepping into a gym. Active wear is never suitable as work attire unless you work in a gym. Manners is about making an effort. As the fashion designer Tom Ford once said, 'Dressing well is a form of good manners.'

AEROPLANE TOILETS

Are disgusting. And, frankly, it doesn't matter what cabin class you're flying in, there always seems to be something on the floor or other surfaces that you'd rather not have identified. Virgin Australia has male and female toilets on many flights, and it's a great idea because men are basically pigs when it comes to bathrooms. I travel a lot in my job, and I have perfected the art of getting in and out of an aeroplane toilet without actually touching any part of it with my fingers. On short flights I refrain from consuming any liquids so that I don't have to use the facilities on board. That said, in-flight life would be much easier if people had more respect for their fellow passengers and left the aeroplane toilet in the state in which they would like to find it.

Nina Katchadourian is an Armenian-American artist who takes photos of herself in aeroplane toilets and uses the paper toilet-seat covers as costumes to depict various famous paintings. It's kind of amusing, but when I first saw her photographs my immediate thought was, I bet there was a line of people outside wondering what on earth the person in there was doing that was taking so long. Airlines are always looking for ways to make their businesses more profitable and one of them is to get as many seats on board as possible. Having fewer toilets on board is one way to do that. All of which means there is more pressure on the remaining toilets – so don't waste time in there creating a Flemish masterpiece. Do what you have to do and get out.

As for sex in aeroplane toilets; personally I think it's an urban myth as I have never seen two people enter or exit a toilet on an aircraft. If I'm wrong, then all I can say is make it quick.

AMERICANISMS

Don't use Americanisms unless you're an American. A lot of these phrases are just management speak these days but they have started to move outside of workplace jargon and have found their way into everyday speech. In real life they make you sound like a twerp, unless you're actually from North America, in which case they make you sound like an American.

I appreciate that the English language is fluid and evolves over time, but some things can actually be said far more eloquently using a more traditional expression. 'Can you do me a solid?' A solid what? A solid is something I do in the privacy of my own home with the door closed. What's so hard about asking, 'Can you do me a favour?' 'Thanks for reaching out.' The only person who reaches out is Diana Ross (and she also touches someone's hand when she does it). Instead of 'deplane the aircraft', try disembarking. 'Touch base' has more or less crept into the way Australians speak, particularly in business environments, and it would be great if it could creep back out again. 'You do the math' should be 'You do the maths' – it's only one extra letter. Some Americanisms can also make you sound a little rude. 'Can I get a . . .' should be 'Can I [or, to be even more polite, May I] have a . . .' One is a demand and the other is a request. And just like I have done in this book, you put things in alphabetical order, you don't alphabetise them.

See also SLANG.

APOLOGISING

This is a story about how one small thing can ruin your whole day, or how one full glass of shiraz can leave you seething in anger for months, possibly years.

You've had a hard and stressful day at work, and you agree at the last minute to meet some friends for a casual dinner (even though you'd much rather go home and sit motionless in front of the television). You secure a table at a busy no-bookings restaurant, drinks are being drunk and dinner is on its way. Your mood lifts and you think to yourself what a great idea this was and how much you're enjoying yourself. Then, while gesticulating wildly, someone accidentally flicks a full glass of red wine – which for some reason is placed on the table to her left – straight into your lap.

What looked like a small amount of wine when it was in the glass suddenly feels like an entire oak cask of the stuff when you're wearing it. To make matters worse, you're wearing light-coloured trousers – and why not, they're in fashion and, besides, you need to break out of only ever wearing navy or charcoal grey to work – and it looks like you're in need of serious medical attention. It's on your expensive bag, which you've miraculously managed to keep away from such incidents for about ten years, as well as on your custom-made suede shoes. And you don't even drink red wine, which is hardly the point but somehow it only serves to make matters worse.

Worse still is the person who committed what you are now thinking must surely be an actual crime. She laughs it off, offers a cursory 'sorry' and continues to tell the story she was telling. You use every available napkin on the table to soak up as much of it from your person as you can, as well as the puddles that are still dripping off the table. Meanwhile, madam continues to brush off the incident – which is easy when you're the dry one – much to the astonishment of the other people at the table, as well as the waiter who has come to your aid. 'Oh, don't worry,' she says, 'it will wash out.' Then – and this is where it gets difficult to remember exactly what was said because you are literally ropeable (in the sense that the only thing that could calm you would be being tied down with a rope) – there is something uttered about soda water and the fact that there are worse things that could happen to you.

To be fair, yes, you could be hit by a bus. But this is dinner in a restaurant and, short of dying from food poisoning, there is actually not anything worse that can happen. Okay, maybe the roof could cave in and kill everyone instantly. But when it comes to wine spilled into your lap, here is the ten-point breakdown of what should have happened:

1. Drink is spilled.
2. The requisite shock, grief, embarrassment, shame and admission of guilt is expressed by the perpetrator. Typically this should consume about ten seconds of time and effort.

3. Napkins are offered to help clean up. You don't actually have to help the victim clean themselves, especially if the beverage has fallen into their swimsuit area, but presenting as many clean napkins as you can reach will go a long way, particularly if you are responsible for the spill.
4. An offer to pay for the dry-cleaning is proffered.
5. The offer is graciously acknowledged by the victim and politely refused.
6. 'Are you sure?'
7. 'Yes, don't be silly, it will be fine.'
8. 'I feel terrible, I'm such a klutz.'
9. 'Oh, it could have happened to anyone.'
10. Replacement drink(s) are ordered and a kind of calm is restored.

That's all it takes. I don't know anyone who has ever actually accepted the offer of dry-cleaning reimbursement, because the money is not the point. The dry-cleaning offer is like a dance, a delicate ballet movement. It is offered, acknowledged and refused. Clothes, no matter how expensive or delicate, are made to be worn, and accidents happen. If something is so precious that a bit of red wine will permanently ruin it then don't wear it out of the house. The point of offering restitution to the victim is a way to make amends and, until time-travel is invented, is the universally accepted course of action in such a situation. Once, in a restaurant in New York, a man at the table next to mine managed to spill soda water on my clothes and still offered to pay for dry-cleaning; but then, New Yorkers are obsessed with dry-cleaning.

Offering to take care of the dry-cleaning also helps to defuse a situation that could get ugly and is especially useful when you don't know the person whose day you have now well and truly ruined. An apology is an admission of guilt, and admissions of guilt are hard to argue with. A simple but heartfelt apology can nullify a situation that is potentially toxic, especially when alcohol is involved.

ASKING SOMEONE THEIR AGE

Ask yourself this: why do you need to know? Asking anyone other than a child how old they are is unnecessary and can easily cause offence. In a work environment it may lead to an accusation of age discrimination, and socially it just makes you look nosy. Even the ever-so-polite sounding, 'I hope you don't mind my asking, but might I inquire how old you are?' at someone's birthday party is impolite. Again, why do you need to know? If you really want to know someone's age then do some detective work – ask around, do a Google search and see what you can uncover. And if you're the sort of person who doesn't want people to know your real age, first, that's perfectly acceptable, and second, here's a hint (but you've probably already worked this out): don't celebrate the milestone birthdays, as it only gives people an opportunity to start counting again.

B

BAGGAGE CAROUSELS

It's more or less stating the obvious but it is worth getting it out in the open here: no one, and I mean no one, enjoys standing around at the baggage carousel at an airport waiting for their luggage. We all have places we'd rather be. Some of us have important meetings that we're running late for, some want to get a jump on the taxi queue and some people just want to get home for no urgent or pressing reason. Whatever your reason for wanting to get your bag as quickly as possible, there is no excuse for pushing and shoving. Bags are loaded onto the carousel in no particular order (I've been fortunate to travel in first class once or twice and my bags were tagged 'priority' but they still came out last), which means the baggage carousel is a level playing field. The hierarchy of airline seat structures doesn't apply here.

There's no need to crowd around the part of the carousel where the bags emerge in an attempt to get your bags first. Would it really be that bad to wait a few seconds for your bags to travel down the conveyor belt? If someone is struggling to get their bag off then it's only polite to help, especially if your own bag is nowhere in sight. Having said that, there won't always be someone available or willing to help you get your bag off the carousel so the rule about being able to carry your own cabin baggage should also apply to checked baggage – never pack what you can't carry. On some flights, particularly when you've just disembarked a large aircraft like an Airbus A380, there can be a lot of people waiting for bags, so even if you're not in a rush, have your wits about you, get your bag off the carousel and move away as quickly as possible to make the process easier for everyone. And please, check your luggage tag to make sure you have your bag and not someone else's before you leave the airport.

BEACHES

When you run along the sand past someone who is lying down you inadvertently kick sand into their face. Running on the beach is a great way to exercise but you should do it on a part of the beach where people are not sitting. You should also remove your thongs as soon as you hit the sand, especially if it is a crowded beach, as they flick sand in a similar fashion to running. And be careful when shaking out your towel upwind from people – they don't want to be on the receiving end of a dust storm.

Most beaches in Australia have banned smoking, but if you're on a beach that hasn't and you smoke, don't bury your cigarette butts in the sand. The thing about beaches is that the sand shifts around and a butt won't stay buried for long. Find somewhere to dispose of it or put it in a receptacle such as an empty soft drink bottle and dispose of both later. Don't leave your rubbish on the beach – if there's no bin anywhere then take it with you.

BEARDS

I have a beard and have had one of one sort or another for about the past twenty years. In the past couple of years, though, I have let it grow a little longer, mainly because I like the way it looks and have decided that it suits the shape of my head. The experience has taught me a thing or two about the contradictory nature of human behaviour. For example, would any man in his right mind approach a woman he barely knows (or even one he knows well) and say, 'Ooh, I love your hair, can I touch it?' and, before an answer is proffered – which most likely would be along the lines of 'Thank you and no' – jump right in and not only touch but rough up the woman's hairdo, all the while pulling her hair?

Of course not, especially if you value your friendship and your life. But for some reason women have no problem doing this to a man with a bushy beard. The first thing a woman should know about beards – and I specify women, as men, even if they have never had a beard, or can't grow one themselves, already know this – is that they're made of hair and when you pull hair it hurts, and when that hair is on your face it really hurts. Second, depending on the type of beard you have it can take some time in the morning getting it to look perfect and not like you've just crawled out from the jungle, so deliberately messing it up is not going to win you any friends. If you want to touch it, ask first and be very gentle. The same goes with the hair on someone's head. If you meet someone with a full-on afro and want to know what it feels like then ask first and respect the answer.

The other thing I've noticed since letting my beard grow is most men think it looks 'awesome' and women are divided into one of two camps: they either love it or they hate it, with no in-between. As a beard-wearer let me assure you that I don't care if you don't like it. There are lots of things I don't like about other people's grooming. For instance, I dislike top knots on women unless they are working out at the gym and I don't like dyed hair on a man in any situation, but I don't go around telling people that – at least, not to their faces. I don't say to someone I have just met (or someone I haven't seen in a while and have therefore not been aware of their new hairstyle), 'What on earth is that thing on your head?

It's hideous. You should go and cut it off immediately!' Believe it or not, that is exactly what people will say to a man if they don't like his new beard. When this happens I'm often tempted to hit back with a smartarse reply like, 'I like it and think it looks good, like you probably think that lipstick colour looks good,' but I don't. I just shrug it off, and if I know their partner I secretly encourage him to grow a beard.

A beard should be looked after – that means brushing it before you leave the house in the morning. You should also find a good barber who knows how to trim a beard, and visit regularly to keep it looking sharp. Contrary to what many people think, you don't just stop shaving and never think about it again.

BE NICE

You catch more flies with honey than with vinegar. It's a much overused expression but it is absolutely true. It's far easier to get what you want from someone by using flattery than it is by making demands. Sure, it's a little more time-consuming to be thinking up ways to be nice to people to achieve your ends, but after a while it kind of becomes second nature and it actually saves time in the long run. If you suffer a rejection from being a demanding arsehole then you only have to go back and do the whole thing all over again to get what you want.

It's a fact of life that seems to have been forgotten sometimes. When the Australian Labor Party lost the federal election in a massive defeat in 2013 it caused many party members to reflect on why voters had turned on them so dramatically. The former Labor Attorney-General Nicola Roxon gave a speech (the John Button Memorial Lecture) in which she offered future Labor governments ten points of advice based on what she had learned from her time in government. Number five was 'Be polite and be persuasive.' Or, I would call this, 'Keep yourself nice.' In her speech Roxon said, 'I know I'll be accused of being "Nanny Nicola" here, but it is an age-old rule that needs to be re-imposed. If you don't do this, you lose ground for no political purpose. You waste time apologising and you lose arguments for no good reason. And this is not a tip just for the sake of nice manners. It fundamentally affects political outcomes too.' So, if you want to succeed in business and in life, then try not to be an arsehole.

BILLS IN RESTAURANTS

These days it's easy for a restaurant to allow patrons to split the payment of a bill over several credit cards. In most cases you should split the bill evenly between the number of guests. Don't make the restaurant do all the maths for you. Work out how much it will cost each person, including a tip, and then hand all the credit cards to the waiter and say you want $100 on each card. If for some reason someone didn't consume any alcohol and everyone else drank like it was an Olympic sport, then consider offering the non-drinker some kind of concession – chances are that person will be the one giving many of you a lift home. Apart from situations like that, dividing the bill evenly is the way to go. Working out what each person paid and getting them to pay for exactly that is a waste of time. First, it almost always comes out almost the same as dividing it evenly and, second, it's a practice you grow out of when you leave university and become gainfully employed.

If you are shouting everyone dinner then sort out the bill away from the table. There's a few reasons for this. It won't embarrass anyone into offering to contribute because the deal is already done. People will look at the bill and may feel embarrassed no matter how much it cost. It can also turn a generous gesture into something that becomes an argument and sours the evening. I don't do it often – I'm a journalist, not a banker – but when I do I quietly inform the restaurant when I arrive, and after dessert is served I excuse myself to go to the bathroom and settle the bill on the way back. If you're fortunate to be on the receiving end of someone's generosity in a restaurant then it's a nice gesture to offer to cover the tip.

BOARDING AN AEROPLANE

I thought everyone knew this, but judging by the behaviour of people in a queue to board a plane perhaps they don't: if you have checked in to your flight it is not going to take off without you, at least not until the airline has made several announcements in the terminal looking for you. There is no need to push. Everyone has an assigned seat so it's not like you will be left standing. Let people with small children and the elderly board first as they are going to take longer to seat than other people and you will just be held up in the aisle or on the aerobridge anyway.

Have your boarding pass out ready to be scanned, not tucked away at the bottom of your hand luggage. If you're wearing a backpack then take it off your back before you board the plane as, when you get on the plane, which is a confined space, you risk knocking someone who is already in their seat in the head with your backpack.

A plane is not only a confined space, it's also one that flies, which makes many people nervous and tense – you don't need to make that worse by jumping an otherwise orderly queue or invading someone's personal space with your belongings.

BODY ODOUR

I used to work in an office where one of my colleagues had the most unbelievable body odour. You could actually still smell him after he'd left the room and you would know when he was in your vicinity without having to look up from your work. The people who worked with me during this time will know exactly who I am talking about. He seemed like a fairly friendly kind of person, although I never got close enough to him to find out for sure (mercifully, I don't think I ever shared a lift with him either). He was also a senior member of staff, which is possibly why no one ever brought the issue up with him, or, if they did, he didn't act on it. Because our brains adjust to smells very quickly, most people cannot actually smell themselves. That's why you should politely let someone know if they, well, stink. I would certainly want to know, if only out of fear that people have been talking about the issue behind my back. But how exactly do you tell someone they smell bad?

Let me demonstrate with another example. Once, I was on a flight back to Sydney from Hong Kong and as the passenger next to me took his seat I was overcome with the pungent aroma of his body odour. The problem with this issue on an aeroplane is that you're stuck next to this person for hours with no escape. So once we were airborne I asked one of the flight attendants if I could move to another seat. The flight attendant told me the flight was full and asked me what was wrong with my assigned seat. I told him and, without missing a beat, he said to leave it with him. I returned to my seat and moments later the flight attendant approached my fellow passenger and quietly spoke to him, and offered him a roll-on deodorant. It turns out flight attendants have to deal with this issue all the time. Later I asked him what he said to the man and he told me he just tells people that, for the comfort of other passengers, they might want to use this, then hands them the deodorant.

It's somewhat easier to handle the situation in this fashion if you don't have to see that person on a daily basis, but in the workplace it needs to be dealt with more diplomatically so as not to cause offence. If you feel that you have a good rapport with the person in question then find a moment to have a quiet chat and just say something like, 'You probably don't realise this, and I would certainly want someone to tell me if it was the case, but you have a slight body odour issue.' Then perhaps make a deodorant recommendation. Always make the problem seem like a minor one and never tell the person exactly how bad the situation is or that it's a topic of conversation in the office.

Or you could take the coward's way out, which is sometimes just as effective. A co-worker once described to me the filthy state of the workstation of the colleague who sat next to him and how much it smelled. It was littered with half-eaten lunches, gym clothes and all manner of garbage. So one day he left a bottle of air freshener and another of fabric deodoriser on his colleague's desk. No note, just the products. You could try the same tactic when it comes to body odour. Just leave a deodorant on your co-worker's desk and hope that they get the message and use it.

Most people don't want to smell bad, but there are others who take it to the extreme and wear too much deodorant or perfume. It's quite possible that this person is unaware of how powerful their scent is as they have become used to it. If the situation is so bad that you need to say something to the heavy fragrance wearer, then use the same amount of tact you would handling someone with body odour. Take the person aside, tell them as a friend and don't make a public scene of it.

Bad breath should also be handled in the same way. If I had bad breath I would want someone to tell me, hopefully before it becomes a much bigger problem and a source of gossip. Be friendly and use your empathetic skills. Take the person aside and say something like, 'You might not be aware of this, but you seem to have a slight breath problem at the moment.' Make the problem sound small, and be a friend and help them out. 'I sometimes get that too, and I've found the best thing to do is to floss more.' Or if the problem is really bad then recommend a visit to the dentist.

Issues around bodily smells are embarrassing for the person who has the smell and really need to be handled with care. If you don't know the person very well or think they will be upset if you speak to them about something so personal, then perhaps it's best to let the matter rest and just live with the smell.

BOOT CAMP

By boot camp I'm referring to groups of people who train with a personal trainer in a public park. Most parks and councils have regulations around the use of the park for private purposes such as personal training, and if you are a trainer or a trainee then you should acquaint yourself with them. Groups of people training in a park or on a beach can irk some of the other people who use the park, for two reasons: first, personal training of this nature is often done early in the morning and, generally speaking, people who get up early in the morning enjoy the peace and quiet that comes with it – personal training in large groups is noisy. And it's an annoying noise – all that yelling and 'more, more' and 'another one' and 'keep it up' is not the way a lot of people want to begin their day. Second, boot camp training is usually done in large groups, and large groups of exercisers are obtrusive and overbearing. So if you are in one of these groups or are the leader of the group be mindful that other people are also trying to enjoy the great outdoors. Don't yell at them to 'look out' as you come charging along the beach. *You* look out. And a flight of stairs, while a handy tool for intensive training, is also a method of getting from A to B, so please don't tell me to watch out as a group of you come charging down the stairs – keep to one side instead. And clean up your mess – empty drink bottles, et cetera – when you leave.

BOW TIES

If you wear one, don't play with it – it only draws attention to the fact that you're not accustomed to wearing one. Or maybe that it's too tight, in which case loosen it.

Whether you should tie a bow tie yourself or wear a pre-tied one isn't such a big deal these days. Many high-end men's fashion brands that you would expect to only sell standard bow ties actually sell pre-tied ones. I think it has something to do with wanting to control the look of their clothes so much that they would prefer to tie it for you rather than have one of their customers make a poor fist of it.

A bow tie looks best with a shirt that has a placket covering the buttons.

BRINGING A PLATE

If you ask people to bring a plate to a pot luck dinner it's a good idea to specify what kind of dish you would like them to bring. No one wants a dinner of eight pear and parmesan salads. You don't need to be too specific – as in you don't need to tell someone to make Kylie Kwong's crispy-skin duck (unless you're inviting Kylie Kwong) – just ask them to bring a salad, or a dessert, or a casserole and let them decide what to make – you want a dish prepared with love rather than resentment.

If you are bringing a dish and it's going to be a big party then consider taking your food in a receptacle that doesn't need to be returned, such as a large foil tray. It saves the host having to wash up a whole lot of dishes and means that if you have a fun night and a few too many drinks you don't need to worry about remembering your best Le Creuset on the way home.

If you take something to someone's house then take something that is ready to go; don't take something that needs complicated preparation just before it's served. Chances are there will be limited space in the kitchen, which is why you were asked to bring something in the first place – you weren't invited to prepare a meal at someone's house. If someone brings a plate of food to your house and it's in a dish or container that needs to be returned, then wash it before you return it. If it's your dish and you left it there then make an effort to collect it as soon as possible – no one wants to store your dish for months on end.

C

CANCELLING PLANS

If you have to cancel something, don't leave it until the last minute. I once had someone text me to say they couldn't make it to dinner as they 'weren't feeling well' at 6 pm, by which time I had bought all the food and done most of the preparation. Give people plenty of notice and offer an explanation and, most importantly, an apology. Don't just text and say you're not feeling well and can't make it, apologise for any inconvenience caused (especially if you want to be invited back again). A text message is fine, by the way. In fact it's probably preferred by the host, who is no doubt busy cooking and tidying their house, so the last thing they want to do is have a lengthy telephone call.

If you are cancelling on an event that involved the purchasing of tickets, then try to find someone to go in your place or offer to reimburse the person who bought the tickets. Sometimes you need to buy tickets to an event such as a concert months in advance, and sometimes your plans change – you might suddenly have to travel for work, for example. Give the organiser as much time as possible to find someone to go in your place and offer to help them do that. If they can't find someone then covering the cost of the ticket is your responsibility. If you're the person who bought the tickets it's a good idea to send a calendar note to the people you bought the ticket for so it will automatically be entered into their diary.

If you made a booking at a restaurant and you can no longer make it then ring the restaurant as soon as you can to cancel it. Restaurants often don't accept bookings because people don't show up after they've made one and it makes the whole process of table reservations impossible to manage. If, like me, you would like more restaurants to take bookings, then make their lives easier and cancel if your plans change. And if you make a booking and plan to keep it then turn up at the restaurant on time.

If the event that you can no longer attend is a group event it's relatively easy to minimise the inconvenience caused (such as offering to pay for your ticket or finding someone to go in your place), but when it was an event with just you and one other person, cancelling is going to have an impact on the other person and, in my opinion at least, you ought to have a good and legitimate excuse, especially if you're doing it at on the day of the event. You should also offer to reschedule and make it up to the person. When it comes to offering an excuse, honesty is the best policy in today's social media age. Telling someone you've changed your mind about going to the movies with them because you've had a crap day and you won't be much company anyway won't earn you any sympathy if the person you're cancelling on sees you at another event later that evening thanks to the marvels of Facebook. You might think you won't be caught out if you don't post anything yourself, but you can't control what other people post. If you want to cancel an outing with a friend, putting it off until the last minute won't spare their feelings – do it as soon as you've changed your mind.

Big events such as weddings and group holidays require a lot of organisation and they rely on people making a commitment. Sometimes things happen that are beyond your control and were unforeseeable at the time of accepting an invitation, and sometimes they happen at the last minute. Even if the reason you have to cancel is beyond your control you need to apologise profusely and offer to cover any costs associated with your cancelling. It's not enough to just say, 'Sorry, I have to go away for work next week and can't come to your wedding anymore.'

But what if I've just changed my mind?, I hear you ask. The key to making a commitment with a friend is not changing your mind. It's not an excuse, it's just bad manners.

CHAMPAGNE

I love a good glass of Champagne, and in my job as the editor of a luxury lifestyle magazine I have had the good fortune to consume more than my fair share of it. I've also met quite a few people who work in the Champagne industry, and the following is based on my conversations and interviews with them.

Australians are big consumers of Champagne – and to be clear, when we refer to Champagne we're talking about sparkling wine that was produced in the Champagne region of France and imported to Australia. Everything else is just sparkling wine. We've become accustomed to drinking Champagne in the same way that we consume cocktails: as a pre-dinner or party drink. This is no doubt due to the expensive nature of this particular wine. But at formal dinners, in the early party of the twentieth century at least, it was viewed as an excellent dinner-party wine. So don't be alarmed if you are served it with dinner. Traditionally, if it is the only wine to be served that evening, it is served from the very first course onwards. If it is to be served in conjunction with other wines then it is served with the meat, or main, course.

Champagne is served either in flutes or, less commonly, in shallow coupe-shaped glasses. To open

Champagne, cover the top of the bottle with a cloth napkin or tea towel and hold it by the top of the neck so the cork is in the palm of your other hand. Turn the cork back and forth a few times and it should release. The napkin is there to stop the cork from shooting out and to prevent any spillage. While it might look like fun, shaking a bottle to pop the cork across the room is in very poor taste and, frankly, stupid. I'd much rather drink it.

When you pour wine into a wineglass the correct way to do it is to leave the glass on the table and, holding the bottle from the bottom, reach towards the glass and fill it in one swift movement, without the bottle touching the rim of the glass. The wine should also not 'chug' as it comes out of the bottle. It's a manoeuvre that requires great skill and a lot of practice, and when I worked in restaurants we used to practice with old wine bottles filled with water. To pour Champagne into a flute, however, it's perfectly acceptable to pick up the glass in your hand and tilt it. The Champagne will fizz to the top quite quickly; return the glass to the upright position and fill the rest of the glass when the fizz has settled.

Champagne should be served cold. If you've forgotten to put it in the fridge you can place it in the freezer for fifteen minutes, but set the timer on your smartphone to remind you to take it out again, as the result of freezing it is a bugger to clean up and a waste. One of the best ways to chill a bottle of Champagne, however, is with a Champagne bucket. The bucket should be made from metal rather than glass as metal will keep the contents cooler longer. Fill the bucket with equal quantities of ice and water, leaving enough space to fit the bottle in. Place the bottle into the bucket and leave it for twenty to thirty minutes, by which time it will have reached the optimum drinking temperature. The combination of water and ice will cause the outside of the bucket to perspire, so if your Champagne bucket doesn't have a drip tray use a dinner plate with a folded napkin on it to absorb the moisture, or you may risk damaging your furniture.

CHILDREN IN RESTAURANTS

It's important to remember that restaurants and cafes are social places where people go to enjoy a meal or a drink, have a break from the pressures of their day or to meet with friends and converse. They don't go there to hear children screaming at the top of their lungs while their parent(s) carry on oblivious to what is happening around them. I'm not a parent, but I was a child once and I know that children are easily bored. How about taking something with you so your child can amuse themselves without annoying fellow restaurant patrons? A book, maybe? Or an iPad with headphones? Never assume that the person at the next table is amused by your child's antics, no matter how cute they seem to you. If your child is screaming their head off then perhaps take them outside and try to calm them. If your children are running around like they're at the playground and won't respond to your repeated requests for them to behave, then perhaps it's time to request the bill. Restaurants and cafes are not free child-minding services so you shouldn't assume that the waitstaff will come to the rescue if your child wanders off while you're busy talking to someone.

Cafes and restaurants are businesses, and the owners of such businesses have to make money to pay their staff wages and keep the doors open. Restaurants don't make much money from children – they don't consume alcohol, which is a big profit driver, and the margin on a babycino is negligible. So if your child leaves a stonking big mess on the table and puts their grubby hands all over the windows, or empties the sugar dispenser to 'draw' with it, then it's really only fair that you leave a decent tip. Or offer to clean up the mess – but in a lifetime of eating in restaurants, and a significant amount of time working in them, I have never seen a parent offer to do that. Restaurants and cafes also make no money from parents who bring their child's meal with them. If you do bring a sandwich with you for your child to eat then politely ask the waitstaff if they don't mind before you bring it out. If they leave bits of it all over the table then clean it up before you leave.

I'm not going to wade into the quagmire about whether or not it's acceptable to breastfeed at a restaurant table; there are people more qualified than me to weigh in on that discussion. Personally it doesn't offend me, and if it means that a screaming child's mouth will be occupied doing something else then I'm all for it. I will, however, say this: never, ever, no matter what the circumstances, change a baby's nappy at the table. I've seen it happen and for the life of me I can't think of a single acceptable justification for it.

There are times, however, when it comes to children in restaurants that it's a case of buyer beware. There is a new cafe just up the road from where I live and the food and coffee there is excellent. Despite this I have only been there once as the establishment seems more like a creche than a cafe. I didn't realise it the time I went (although, in hindsight, the queue of high chairs at the entrance should have been a clue) but I made a mental note not to go there again if I wanted to eat in peace and quiet. There's no point in getting frustrated by a situation when you're the odd one out. But just as one shouldn't assume that a restaurant will preference child-free patrons over families, you shouldn't just assume that a restaurant will be set up to cater to young guests. If you need a high chair and the restaurant takes reservations then inform them at the time of booking. Similarly, ask if they have a child's menu. If you arrive at a cafe and there is no room for your pram, ask the staff where they would like you to store it – they will know the best place for it so it's out of everyone's way.

CHILDREN ON AEROPLANES

I have a friend who recently had an incident on a flight regarding a noisy child. Here's a summary: he was in business class, as was a family of five – two adults and three children. One child was particularly noisy and kept him and everyone else in the cabin awake with screaming. At a certain point in the flight the child, who was also somewhat restless, spilt water on my friend while he was trying to sleep. He got enraged, said something to the parents in the heat of the moment and stormed off to the toilet, only to very quickly regret his actions.

Here are a few realities about plane travel: children travel, they can be noisy, their noise and misbehaviour annoys their parents as well as fellow passengers, and some parents can afford to fly with their children in business class – meaning money doesn't buy you immunity to travelling with a noisy child. Unfortunately you do have to grin and bear it for the most part, especially if the child is a baby or a toddler under the age of about two. In my experience parents try very hard to keep their kids well behaved but when it comes to a baby it is out of their control to a certain degree. Older children, however, can be disciplined by their parents and if a child who is old enough to know better is making too much noise, or kicking the back of your seat or invading your personal space, then it's perfectly acceptable to mention it politely to the child's parent.

If you are the parent then you should be mindful of what your children are doing and the impact they are having on other passengers.

If children really bother you then you should ask to be seated away from children if possible when you check in to your flight.

I've been seated near some annoying children on flights but I've also been seated way too close to some very annoying adults as well – I'm thinking of you, sir, the one who clipped his toenails in his seat then put the clippings on his tray table and rubbed antifungal cream into his feet. Then there was the man who had such bad BO that I had to drug myself to sleep with sedatives to avoid it, and in the process injured my back from sleeping in an awkward position. Or there was the woman who wanted to tell me her life story even when I had headphones on. The list is endless, so, suffice to say, there are times on flights when I'd be happy to trade a pesky adult for an unsettled child.

CHOPSTICKS

Chopsticks are picked up with the right hand and the tips placed in the left hand. Then the fingers of your right hand slip under the ends of the chopsticks about two-thirds of the way up and hold them open. The higher up the chopsticks you place your fingers demonstrates how skilled you are, and in Asian cultures it often signifies your social class. Peasants, who might frequently eat with their hands, hold chopsticks closer to the tips. To use the chopsticks, anchor the lower one firmly against the fourth (ring) finger, moving only the upper one freely. Open and close the tips to pick up bite-sizes pieces – don't spear food with a chopstick. Using chopsticks well requires practice, and if you think you might make a hash of it then ask for a knife and fork.

Chopsticks are traditionally used with the right hand even if you are left-handed. Although biases against left-handed eaters are less prevalent today, in some formal Chinese restaurants the practice of using them in the left hand might be frowned upon as poor etiquette. In most restaurants, people probably won't notice so long as you are using them correctly.

COMPLIMENTS

Specifically, how to accept one. If someone pays you a compliment you should accept it and not knock it back. I'm terrible at it and tend to brush off a compliment in a self-deprecating manner and try to be funny about it, but that can get annoying after a while, and people may decide it's too hard to pay you a compliment, and stop altogether. I have, however, watched other people do it and the clever ones just accept it graciously. If someone tells you that you look nice today, all you have to say in return is, 'Thank you, that's very kind of you to say.' If someone pays you a compliment for something you had no hand in other than choosing it – such as a really great pair of shoes or item of clothing – you can accept the compliment by saying something like, 'Thanks, I'm glad you like them, I thought they were really cool.' Where people get stuck is they think you have to offer a compliment in return, and you don't, because when you do it will look forced and as though you are only doing it because the person said something nice about you. You can return the compliment at a later date when it is unexpected.

While it's nice to give and receive compliments, you should avoid becoming the person who gives them so indiscriminately that they lack sincerity. You should also avoid hyperbole. I once received a compliment from a co-worker who told me how nice I looked and that I was the best-dressed man in the office. I didn't really believe her, but I accepted the compliment graciously. A few minutes later I overheard her say more or less the same thing to another male in the office. I've never believed a thing she's said to me since.

Compliments shouldn't just be about someone's dress or personal appearance. Compliment someone if they're skilled at reverse parking, or can cook a nice meal, or if they've done a good job at work, even if you're not their boss.

COMPUTER DESKTOPS

The company I work for sets our computer desktop background for us and it can't be overridden or changed.

If, however, you have the freedom to set your own desktop background image then choose wisely. I once went to a meeting at the office of a potential advertiser for the magazine I edit, and when the colleague who was responsible for putting together our presentation plugged his laptop into the projector system and opened his laptop, up popped a giant photo of him in a pair of speedos at the beach. Sure, if I was as fit and handsome as him I would be showing off my body too, but there is a time and place for it, and, judging by the reaction of the other people in the room that day, this was not it. Even if you don't use your work computer for doing presentations you should keep your desktop background G-rated.

CONDOLENCE MESSAGES

Can you send someone a text as a condolence message? Yes you can, if you know that person is okay with text messaging in general. Speaking from experience, I actually think a text is more personal than an email in this situation and it also means the sender doesn't have to think about something long-winded to say in order to take up space. People often don't know what to say in a condolence message and a two-line email always looks a bit short to me, but a text is meant to be short, so simply sending something like, 'Dear X, I'm so sorry to hear about [name], I just wanted to let you know that I'm thinking of you and if there is anything at all that I can do, please don't hesitate to ask. Love, X.' That message gets the job done and is delivered directly into the hands of the intended, whereas a written note may not. So many times I've heard people say, 'I would have called but I didn't know what to say', or 'I would have called but I didn't know if it was appropriate.' A text gets around both of those problems.

A text is best when you first hear the news, and following up with a written condolence note later is a nice touch, but one doesn't cancel out the other. The written note is where you can put a few more thoughts down if you think it's appropriate. A text message also means the person who is grieving doesn't have to have endless telephone conversations hearing the same platitudes over and over, which can be excruciating when you are in that situation.

When my father died, a few relatives and family friends that we don't see all that often provided anecdotes for use in his eulogy, and also sent old photos of him – some from before he was married and, as such, before we knew him, and some taken by relatives when my siblings and I were young children. Seeing the photos brought back great memories. In the last few years I have had a couple of friends pass away and when it happens I've gone through boxes of old photos to find memories of them. If I find a nice photo of one of my friends with the deceased I scan it and email it to the friend as a reminder of how wonderful this friend of ours was. I think it's a nice gesture, and modern technology has made it very easy to do and for you to be able to keep the original photo. No one has ever told me they didn't want to see a photo that I had sent.

CONFERENCE CALLS

Conference calls can be a productive way of working with people who are not in the same city as you but they can also end up being a waste of time if they're not well organised, and sometimes a group email or a series of individual phone calls might prove to be more productive. As the organiser you need to be mindful of the different time zones people are in and organise a mutually convenient time for everyone, not just you. Send everyone an agenda in advance so people know what will be discussed, as well as the names and positions of the various people on the call in case not everyone knows each other. On the day, make sure the technology is working properly ahead of time, especially if you will be having a video call. For conference-call meetings you really need someone to be in charge and steer the conversation. People should try to speak one at a time and not over the top of each other. When the call begins everyone should say their names themselves rather than be introduced by one person, as that way the people not in the room will be able to associate a particular voice with a name. Then, when you contribute something to the meeting, say your name again. If you're on a conference call and you're the only person not in the meeting room – that is, you're the person on the end of the line – then be aware that sometimes the multi-directional microphone designed for conference calls can be very powerful and pick up all manner of sounds, such as the *click-click-click* of you typing on your phone or the sound of you flicking through a magazine. Yes, conference calls can be dull when you're the only one not in the room, but don't give the game away that you're not giving the discussion your undivided attention.

COOKING FOR OTHER PEOPLE

When you invite people to your house for dinner you don't need to prepare the most elaborate gourmet meal in order to impress them. For busy people, any amount of effort is usually appreciated. Learn to do a few things well and keep doing them. People are genuinely impressed if you can make a cake from scratch and if they see that sitting on a cake stand when they arrive it immediately tells them you've gone to some trouble.

If you make a mean lasagne then keep making it – people will remember you for it and probably be looking forward to a repeat performance the next time they are invited around. Pair it with some different side dishes if you want to mix it up a little.

The best dinner parties are the ones where everyone is relaxed. If you're stuck in the kitchen and stressing out about the food then that tense vibe can be contagious. I once had a group of people over for dinner, one of whom was a well-known chef. I decided to make something I had made many times before so the margin of error would be narrow. It was a recipe for fish curry by Charmaine Solomon. When it was time to serve the meal my chef friend came into the kitchen to help me. 'Okay, where's the rice, I'll dish that up,' she said. My face went white. Not only had I not cooked the rice, there wasn't even any in the house – I totally forgot to buy it. We both ended up on the floor laughing as the other guests looked on. Luckily there was a supermarket across the road and the meal was saved. When something like this happens, refill everyone's glasses and keep the good mood light while you regain your composure in the kitchen.

Your guests will always gravitate towards the kitchen; that's what human beings do, they gather around the hearth. The way to keep them out of the kitchen, especially if it's small and cramped, is to have a distraction for them. Set up a bar area somewhere away from the kitchen that is well stocked with ice, mixers and glassware. If you can have someone tend the bar and serve people, that's great. If not, set it up so people can serve themselves and won't need to enter the kitchen for anything other than to say hello.

When your guests arrive, come out of the kitchen to greet them – another good way to keep them out if you don't want them in the way is to leave the kitchen when they enter and draw their attention to someone or something in the room. You could also ask one of your guests to be on kitchen patrol and keep other people away while you're working.

COVERT PHOTOS

We've all seen them. They're those photos that some smartypants posts to Twitter or Instagram, pretending to take a selfie but really focusing on the person in front of them in a queue who has a hideous amount of butt crack showing. Not only are these photos cowardly – if you don't have the guts to take the photo honestly, then don't take it at all – they're just making fun of someone less fortunate than themself, and are therefore not clever, just plain mean. Yes, some people wear spectacularly ugly things out of the house, or just plain weird things, but they're not ugly or weird to the person who is wearing them. If you feel that something simply must be recorded for posterity, at least have the decency to tap someone on the shoulder and say, 'I love what you're wearing, can I take a selfie with you?'

CUSTOMER SERVICE

If you're in the customer service business – and most of us are in one form or another, when you think about it – then good manners will go a long way towards getting repeat business. If you work in a shop and someone asks you how much something is, the correct answer is not 'The price is on the box, man.' Granted, it was General Pants Co., but actually telling me the price or looking at the box for me would have endeared me to the salesperson and, by extension, the company, more.

Try to smile with your voice when you're on the telephone – remember, you catch more flies with honey than with vinegar. 'Mr Meagher, could you please call us at your earliest convenience' was the voicemail message I received from an airline the day before a recent flight. It sounded serious, grave even. I assumed the worst – the flight had been cancelled or delayed. So when I called back I was primed for disappointment and a potential argument. It turns out I had been upgraded to business class. A bit of excitement rather than gloom in the caller's voice might have been warranted in this situation. The last thing you want is someone calling you back and launching into a full-on spray because they assume – wrongly, as it happens – that something bad is about to come down the line.

Today a bad customer service experience can result in something a lot more lasting than a call or letter to your boss. People post reviews in online forums that can hurt your business for years to come because they will appear in search results whenever someone searches for your business. Because of this, some companies are on the front foot and actually ask for a positive review, whether it's on an independent website or via their own customer satisfaction survey, at the point of transaction.

I've checked out of a hotel and been asked to give them a positive review on TripAdvisor, had a meal in a restaurant and been asked to do the same and even collected my car from being serviced and been asked to give a good score when I was contacted later in the week about completing a survey. The thing is, you don't ask for a positive score or review, you earn it. And the best way to earn it is to leave people with a positive impression of you and the company you work for.

CYCLING

Many cyclists, it seems to me, want to have their cake and eat it too. They want to be afforded the same rights as motorists and be treated as equals when they cycle on the road, but at the same time they want the freedom to break the law: to go through red lights when it suits them, to go up a one-way street in the wrong direction, exceed the speed limit in some cases, and to talk on a mobile phone while riding. They also want more bike lanes built around the city (I'm referring specifically to Sydney here, but many Australian cities are install-ing bike lanes), but then they don't seem to want to use them. I live on a street that has a bike lane that is separate from both the road and the footpath, but still a significant number of cyclists choose to ride on the footpath or the road. I don't ride a bike so I have no idea about the mentality that says, why not risk my life in the traffic instead of using a purpose-built – and relatively safe – bike lane. I can only assume it's because these cyclists think bike lanes are uncool. I've come to this conclusion because it seems the cyclists who don't like to wear helmets – mandatory in Australia, by the way – are also the ones who don't like to ride on the bike lanes.

Living next to a bike lane also means that I'm witness to daily altercations between cyclists and pedestrians. In fact, now when I hear people yelling outside I don't assume, as I once did, that it is a road rage incident between two drivers, I immediately assume it has something to do with a cyclist and a pedestrian. 'Why don't you ride in the bike lane instead of the footpath?' yelled an angry pram-pushing pedestrian as I was writing this section of the book. 'Why don't you fuck off, you self-righteous bitch?' yelled back the cyclist as he rode away. That was a verbatim exchange, by the way. Talk about the pot calling the kettle black.

I've also been told to fuck off by a cyclist when I casually suggested that they ought to be riding on the bike lane that was less than two metres away from the narrow footpath they were riding on. On this particular occasion I told him off because he rang his bell at me at 5.45 am when I was leaving my house to go running. There was no traffic on the road and none on the bike lane either, so why was he riding on the footpath? 'Is there a problem here?' he asked as I rolled my eyes at him when he rode past. 'Well, now that you mention it, yes there is. There's a bike lane just there, so why don't you use it and I'll use the footpath and everyone will be happy, and you won't have to ring that bell at this hour of the morning?' was my response. 'Why don't you fuck off, the path is there to share.' I give up.

While the law was technically on my side in this instance, the law doesn't really help much at 5.45 am if there is no way to enforce it. In a way this is not an issue of manners, it's about adhering to the rules, and if everyone did that then most of the time there would be no problem. I'm all for the use of bicycles as a mode of transport, and these days people are encouraged to give up car ownership and use bikes and public transport instead. So, in the spirit of 'the road is there to share', here are some rules for cyclists and pedestrians sharing a path:

1. Use the bike lane if there is one.
2. If you're going to ride on the footpath then give way to all pedestrians. A 'shared' path doesn't mean a free-for-all. Cyclists should yield to pedestrians. As a cyclist you should dodge pedestrians and go around them rather than making them go around you. If you don't like that notion then use the road.
3. Go slow; a walking speed would be best. If you want to go faster . . . you guessed it, get on the road.
4. Use your bell the way a driver would use their horn; that is, only when it is necessary. And you don't have to *ding-ding-ding-ding-ding-ding* to signal you're behind someone. Once is enough.

5. Get front and rear lights for your bike so pedestrians and drivers can see you coming at night-time.
6. If there is a sign that says 'dismount at crossing' or similar, then that means you get off your bike and walk it across.
7. If you're walking a dog on a shared path then keep it on a leash and close to you. Long retractable cords can be hard for cyclists and other pedestrians to see.
8. If you jog at night, make sure some part of your clothing is reflective so cyclists can see you.
9. If it's clearly designated a shared path then walk on the left-hand side – with the traffic, in other words.

When riding a bicycle on the road, the first thing to know is that most motorists don't actually want to hit a cyclist. The ones that do are very much in the minority and could be categorised in the same way as murderers are in wider society – they're out there but they are not the majority of people. Here's another way to think about it: most drivers don't want to hit a cyclist if only because they don't want to do damage to their car and go through the whole rigmarole of fixing it and fixing the cyclist. I realise that sounds callous, but it's the truth – no one wants a collision. Accidents do happen, and we will get to how to deal with that later. With that in mind, here are some rules for cyclists and motorists sharing the road:

1. You live by the sword, you die by the sword. So if you want to ride your bike on the road then you must obey the traffic laws. Traffic rules are designed to avoid accidents, and when everyone knows the rules and obeys them you can have an informed idea about what the vehicles around you are doing. It's like a sixth sense; you can anticipate what the car in front, behind or beside you is going to do based on what the law dictates they should do, and then react accordingly. If you flout the laws when you're on a bike you make it very hard for drivers to predict what you're doing, and you're almost inviting an accident or a near miss. So, look up what the rules are for riding a bike on the road, learn them and then stick to them.

2. The same applies for motorists: know the road rules as they pertain to cyclists and how cars should interact with them on the road. Don't try to intimidate a cyclist by driving close to them or overtaking them unnecessarily. It's not the cyclist's fault that you're running late.

3. If you're one of those people who ride their bike in a pack – you know, the ones who wear matching lycra outfits – then you need to be aware that a group of ten or more cyclists riding together in a pack is like a slow-moving bus or a semitrailer to a motorist. Wave the car past if it's safe for them to pass (in other words, if you plan on remaining in a pack). Cyclists should also stick to the speed

limit. And neither cyclists nor motorists should be aggressive, as it just invites more aggression.

4. Motorists and passengers in vehicles should always look when opening a car door and before you get out of your car.

5. Use you indicators – that applies to motorists and cyclists.

6. Try to keep your cool. Near misses will happen, and the operative word here is 'miss'. A near miss is unpleasant and your mind will naturally race to what might have happened. But if nothing bad did happen then it's best to learn from your mistakes, as a driver or a cyclist, and move on. If you're the motorist in a near miss (in other words, the larger and more dangerous object) then a wave of apology would be a good gesture to defuse a situation that could otherwise turn ugly very quickly. If no persons and no property were damaged and a motorist admits complete responsibility – 'I'm so sorry, I just didn't see you coming, my apologies,' – it's hard to argue with that.

As I said, I'm basing this on my observations from living on an inner city street with a bike lane for the last few years. There are some intersections in my part of Sydney where accidents are waiting to happen. One in particular is so bad that when turning right as a motorist you need to give way to pedestrians on a pedestrian crossing, then a two-lane bike lane and *then* the traffic on the road, and by the way, all that traffic is coming from around a bend. At this particular inter-section – and there are many others like it – it is virtually impossible to see what's coming without making an attempt to turn. Until traffic lights are installed here the only way through is to gingerly make your attempt and hit the brakes when you see a car or bike coming, and then try again when they've passed. After I nearly hit someone on a bike recently I made a complaint to the council and the response I got was comical in its stupidity. The person I spoke to at the council told me I should take an alternative route. When I pointed out that it won't fix the problem, he responded that at least it won't be me who hits someone.

D

DESK ETIQUETTE

You should keep your desk as neat and tidy as possible. Depending on what your job is this can be a challenge, but if you share a pod with people one untidy desk can ruin the ambience of the entire pod. Not long ago I bought a new car and when I went into the salesman's office to do the deal, I was taken aback by how tidy his desk was. There was nothing on it apart from his telephone and his computer – not a scrap of paper, or a pen or a stack of Post-it notes. His desk seemed huge and I couldn't help but ask how long he'd been in this office. I fully expected him to say he'd just moved in, as no one can keep their desk this spartan. 'A tidy desk is a tidy mind' was his answer. It was impressive and I envied him, mainly because I find it impossible to keep my desk tidy, certainly not as tidy as his anyway.

If you have to occasionally meet with people at your desk then try to keep it as tidy and clean as possible. Remove dirty coffee cups and clean off any rings they have left on the tabletop. If you eat at your desk, throw the remains in the rubbish as soon as you're done and sweep up the crumbs. Your children's finger-paintings are terribly cute but they would probably look better on the fridge at home. One or two personal photographs is fine, but any more than that looks like you'd rather be on holidays than at work – of course we would all rather be on a beach somewhere, but the goal here is to convey a semblance of professionalism.

Gym clothes and towels belong in a locker, not hanging on the back of your chair, and if your company doesn't provide lockers then put them in your gym bag. Air them out at home, not in the air that your co-workers have to breathe. Keeping a spare pair of shoes under your desk is fine but don't let your collection get out of hand – it shouldn't look like Imelda Marcos has taken up residence under your desk.

I have a thoughtful colleague who has a bowl of lollies on her desk, which I avail myself of several times a day. If you work with someone as kind and considerate as this then make an effort to occasionally replace their lolly of choice. I don't have such a bowl on my own desk as I don't possess the willpower to consume them gradually. Don't store perishable food at your desk; that goes in the office fridge.

If you borrow something from someone's desk when they are not there – a stapler, pen, phone charger, keyboard, chair – then return it promptly. If you sit at someone's desk for the day when they are out of the office or away on holidays then make sure you leave it as you found it for their return.

If you work in an office that uses a hot-desk system there will no doubt be rules about how you have to leave the desk you use each day. Stick to the rules, and if there aren't any, then follow the time-honoured logic of leaving something in a state in which you would like to find it.

When I was at school we had to tidy our desks at the end of each day before we were dismissed from the classroom. It's a habit I've found hard to break and it does have one advantage – if you tidy your desk before you leave the office each day you will return in the morning to a clean and tidy workplace, which makes starting the day that little bit more pleasant.

See also OPEN-PLAN OFFICES.

DIM SUM OR YUM CHA

I have filed this section under 'D' for dim sum as that's the technically correct term for Chinese dumpling meals served from carts in a restaurant. Yum cha translates as 'drink tea' and is a type of high-tea service where food is also served, a little like the British tradition of afternoon tea, where sandwiches and sweets are served with tea. These days, however, in Western countries the two terms have more or less become interchange-able. Eating dim sum is a great way to enjoy lunch with a large group. Chinese restaurants that service this kind of cuisine are almost always noisy and very busy places. They generally don't take bookings and there is a queuing system. If you have a large party then get there early – if you don't then be prepared to wait and don't try to jump the queue. Dim sum works best when everyone shares dishes, but if there's something that you particularly like and others don't, such as chicken feet, then by all means order it.

Chinese tea is traditionally served with dim sum – remember, that's what yum cha means – and you should pour tea for other people before you pour yourself some. When the tea pot is empty, take out the lid and place it on top of the pot and to the side of the opening to indicate to the waiter, by leaving the top of the pot open, that you would like a refill. In dim sum restaurants waitstaff usually have clearly defined roles – drinks, for example, can only be ordered from the waiters; the people pushing the food trolleys don't take drink orders or arrange your bill for you.

You can ask for a knife and fork in a dim sum restau-rant, but be prepared to get a disapproving look from the waiter when you do. Try to learn how to use chop-sticks if you don't know how – there are plenty of videos on YouTube that demonstrate the technique – but if you just can't master them then there is no harm in asking for a knife and fork. I'd much rather get a disapproving look from a waiter than spill food all over myself. As yum cha is a communal dining experience you need to know the correct way to dip your dumplings into soy sauce. The table is usually set with a small dish for every guest. You place soy sauce in this dish with some chilli or ginger if you wish. If you're in a Taiwanese restaurant where the dumplings are often filled with a broth as well as meat and vegetables, there is a correct way to eat them that will help you avoid getting food down your front. Take one of the dumplings with your chopsticks, dip it in the soy sauce (if desired) then place the dumpling in the deep spoon that should be at your place setting. You prick the dumpling with a chopstick to release the broth, then bring the dumpling to your mouth with the spoon rather than the chopsticks.

The whole experience in a dim sum restaurant can be frenetic, with people talking across a large round table, children running around and screaming, waiters barking orders at other staff members and so on. It's not like a traditional restaurant where everyone is served at the same time and eats courses at more or less the same pace. You should check with the table that everyone has had enough to eat before you ask for the bill.

DINNER PARTIES

See BRINGING A PLATE, FOOD ALLERGIES, HOST OR HOSTESS GIFTS, VEGETARIANISM AND VEGANISM, WHO IS COMING TO DINNER?.

DOGS

Nobody loves your dog as much or thinks your dog is as cute as you do. It's handy to remember that when you're in a park and your dog is begging other people for food or treats. Other dog owners might also find your dog tiresome. Even if your dog wouldn't hurt a fly you should obey rules that stipulate whether a park is off-leash or not.

Always pick up after your dog. It's an unpleasant aspect of owning a dog but it's a reality that you have to pick up their poo. I've had a dog for fourteen years and I've become immune to the hideousness of it. Having said that, my dog is about the size of a small handbag so his poo can be picked up with enough plastic bag left over to create a nice buffer between my hand and the poo. If you are really squeamish about this necessary aspect of dog ownership then I would suggest getting a small dog rather than a Great Dane.

Then there is the issue of urination. I have a male dog who would lift his leg on every street corner, tree or lamppost if I let him. As I live in the inner city I am conscious of not letting him wee on hard surfaces, like the corner of a building or a footpath, as it leaves an unpleasant odour and stain as it dries. It's a constant battle but I try to steer him towards an organic substance such as a tree or a nature strip.

Taking a dog to a friend's house is like taking a child, especially if the person you are visiting doesn't have a dog. If you have a dog that is often restless then you need to take a toy to keep the dog occupied. You should also take something for the dog to drink or eat out of, as some people can be sensitive about allowing dogs to eat from bowls that are meant for humans. Take your dog's bed with you if you can – it will help to keep him off your friend's furniture, and thus avoid an act that could ruin a friendship.

A long leash such as one of those retractable leashes that rolls up into a plastic handle can be convenient if you have a dog that needs to be kept on a leash at all times. At night-time, however, walking a dog on one of those with the leash fully extended is a trip hazard for pedestrians. If your dog wants to pee on every tree he passes on his evening walk then here's an idea – walk him on that side of the footpath to avoid extending your leash – a taut, thin cable – across a darkened walkway.

Dogs sometimes get into fights and if your dog is the aggressor in a fight that ends in an injury (and there's always one who is the clear instigator) then you should make an offer to drive the victim to the vet, if you drive and your car is nearby, and to pay for the vet bills. It happened to me once and the vet's bill was significant. I graciously acknowledged the offer to pay and said it wouldn't be necessary. The owner of the offending dog was a friend of a friend so she knew where I lived and came to visit me a few days later with a peace offering of something for me and something for my dog. Here's a tip: while that's a lovely and kind gesture, perhaps don't bring Cujo with you when you drop the gift around.

Dogs, no matter how domesticated they are, behave like animals sometimes and can harm another dog, uproot an azalea bush or tear washing off the line. If your dog causes destruction you should make an effort to repair the damage or present a peace offering as soon as possible. The dog can't apologise so you need to do so on its behalf.

If your dog barks a lot when you're not home you'll find out soon enough, as your neighbours won't waste any time letting you know. If you're the neighbour then you should give the dog owner the benefit of the doubt that they were unaware of the barking and give them a chance to address the problem. If you're the dog owner there is probably a reason why your dog is barking and you need to work out what that is and do something (cruelty free) about it. Consult the internet as a starting point or speak to your vet. A barking dog is like a screaming baby – no one, not even the parents, want one that screams – and ignoring it won't fix the problem or endear you to your neighbours.

DON'T SPEAK ILL OF THE DEAD

Social media allows everyone to express their opinion about something or someone, and that's not always a great thing. Once upon a time if you wanted to express an opinion in a newspaper you could write a letter to the editor and you would be vetted and edited. Today you can just leave a message on a newspaper's Facebook page or in the comments section at the end of a story. Now you can pass judgement on almost every story and every subject, but you should exercise a degree of civility when it comes to commenting about a person who has recently died. Even if that person was a known scumbag, chances are they have a family to whom they are not a scumbag. Sometimes it's best to keep your thoughts to yourself and say nothing at all.

DRIVING

See CYCLING, ROAD RAGE, ROAD RULES and ZEBRA CROSSINGS.

DROP-IN GUESTS

Everyone likes a surprise visitor but no one wants un-announced drop-in guests. I'm sure you have a mobile phone, so use it. If you happen to be in someone's neighbourhood and you want to see if they're home then call first and give them a few minutes to quickly tidy the house, change their clothes, brush their hair and make sure the bathroom is in a fit state. I don't live in a mansion so I can do all of that in about fifteen minutes – which, by happy coincidence, is also the amount of time it would take for my potential guest to pick up something for afternoon tea.

E

EATING IN THE STREET

There is a simple rule when it comes to eating in public: you don't. Now, obviously a restaurant is a public space, so on that level the rule doesn't make sense, but what I'm really talking about here is walking down a CBD street at lunchtime and eating sushi with chopsticks at the same time (and, yes, I have actually seen someone do that). Not only is that particular example unsightly, it's also downright dangerous. If your meal requires cutlery to eat it then sit down to do so. Then there's the city sandwich-shovelers – you know them, the ones walking through the CBD eating a large sandwich with an abundance of fillings threatening to fall out. Or, even worse, the person doing it while talking on their mobile at the same time. Not only do unsuspecting members of the public have to look at this unsightly mess, but the poor person at the other end of the phone has to have a conversation with someone who is talking with their mouth full.

I certainly appreciate that not everyone has the time to sit down somewhere and consume their lunch in private. But being busy shouldn't be an excuse for bad behaviour. We're all busy. If we just threw out age-old conventions about manners and etiquette, where would we be? Good manners, such as the ones concerned with eating, are what separates us from wild animals. After my first book on manners was published I received a letter from a reader asking me what I thought about 'all these people walking the streets swigging from water bottles'. I have to say that water bottles don't offend me as much as they do others. We all need to keep up our hydration, after all. But the food thing does bother me.

Books on etiquette devote a great number of pages to the business of eating in all manner of social situations. In the name of research I've consumed dozens of historical texts on the subject to try to come up with a modern approach to the issue. If I could summarise everything I have learned about the rituals of consuming food into one sentence, I would say it almost always comes down to making the experience of communal dining pleasant for one's fellow diners. The rule about chewing with your mouth closed, for example, is just so the other people at the dinner table don't have to witness the beginnings of the digestive system (and as an added bonus it prevents food from falling out).

Which brings me back to roaming the streets and eating at the same time. Personally I like to defer to the Japanese, who have very strict rules when it comes to eating in the street, for adjudication on this issue. In Japan, as many tourist guides will tell you, eating while walking is deeply frowned upon. About the only thing permissible to eat while walking in Japan is an ice-cream, for fairly obvious reasons – you need to eat it before it melts.

EATING WHILE TALKING ON THE PHONE

Is really the same as talking with your mouth full. I like eating in restaurants on my own and I do it regularly when I travel. I'm perfectly comfortable with my own company or a book or magazine to entertain me. Or sometimes I just read on my smartphone, catch up on emails or look at social media. What bugs me, however, are fellow diners who think eating alone is a perfect opportunity to catch up on phone calls. It means you not only have to listen to someone speak and chew food at the same time (see SPEAKING WITH YOUR MOUTH FULL), you have to endure them doing it all loudly so the poor person on the other end of the phone can hear them. I say 'poor person' because the sound of someone speaking and eating at the same time is just awful. As with most things in life, doing one thing at a time is always a good idea.

See also TALKING IN A RESTAURANT OR CAFE.

E-CIGARETTES

Restrictions on smoking vary from state to state in Australia and, at the time of writing, the states are in many cases still grappling with exactly how to deal with electronic cigarettes or 'vaping'. In some states, such as Queensland, they are classed as a tobacco product and are subject to the same usage rules. In others, such as Victoria, they are at present unclassified but by mid-2017 will be regarded in the same way as any tobacco product, which means you won't be able to use one anywhere you also can't smoke a regular cigarette, pipe or cigar.

Many workplaces have already set down laws about using them and, for the most part, they are the same as the rules for smoking. In other words, you can't vape at your desk or anywhere else in the building. If your building is classed as 'smoke free' then that will also include vaping. If you want to vape you need to take it outside and be four metres from the entrance to the building.

Even though the law is yet to fully catch up, it's clear the rules that apply to smoking will eventually also apply to e-cigarettes. If you live in a jurisdiction that is still working out what to do about e-cigarettes then perhaps it would be best if you prepare for the inevitable and use them the way you would if you smoked. And even though the law might, strictly speaking, be on your side at this point in time, if you're sitting at an outdoor table in a restaurant and someone at the next table asks you to refrain from vaping in their general direction, be considerate and do it elsewhere.

ELEVATORS

I once spent five hours stuck in a lift full of people, and ever since I've had a fear of getting into crowded lifts. I'd rather take the stairs, if it's only a few floors, or wait for the next lift if there's more than one other person in there.

Lifts are confined spaces – very confined, usually – and therefore some basic rules should be observed in order to make the experience of being in a confined space with complete strangers less uncomfortable. You should offer a cursory greeting to people when you get into a lift that other people are already in. A simple smile or nod will do, but it seems weird to share such a small space with other people and not acknowledge their existence.

Don't crowd the door of a lift while you're waiting for it, so people can get out easily. Similarly, if you're travelling to one of the top floors in a building – or to the ground floor, on the way down – then move to the back of the lift to let others get in and out with ease.

Hold the door for someone if you can see they're not far away – and if someone holds the lift for you then thank them. This action will not kill you or really have much of an impact on your day, except that you might give or receive a grateful smile. If you're running so late that holding a lift for someone is going to cause problems for you then maybe you need to exercise more effective time management.

Once upon a time a man would stand back and let a woman enter or exit a lift first, just as a man would open a door for a woman. It was just good manners, and was more to do with chivalry than sexism. A lot of people today would argue those two are more or less the same thing, or at least that chivalry is rooted in sexism and the belief that women are the fairer and weaker sex. Opening doors and alighting lifts is something I've been asked about many, many times. Should I stand back and let women get out of the lift first? It's a difficult one to answer and technically the answer is yes, but also women and men are equal. So here's what I do: I stand back and let whoever else is getting in or out of the lift at the same floor as me, regardless of gender, get out first. Sure it sometimes leads to a 'no you first, no you first' back-and-forth but at least it gives the impression of politeness.

Then there's the issue of rank. If you're in a lift with your boss you should always allow them to exit the lift first and indicate to them that is what you are doing. If the other person says, 'No you go first, I insist,' don't stand there wasting people's time with a performance about who should get off first, just do it and say thank you to the other person.

Don't break wind in a lift even if you are on your own – you know why.

EMAILS

I'm sure I speak for many people here when I say that emails are the bane of my life. It is the one single thing about my job I wish I could do away with. Remember when you first got an email address and you would hit 'send and receive' every now and then in the hope that someone out there had sent you something? When the technology was so new there was a novelty factor in sending and receiving an email? It was a bit like when you first had access to a fax machine and you would send some bit of scribble to a friend who also had access to one just for the sheer fun of it. Today when I get into work I open up my email application – if I haven't already done so at home – and feel physically ill at the number of new emails that require my attention. The email burden is so great that it fills me with dread just writing this section of the book – I know there are 1500 unread emails in my inbox right now that I could be wading through and responding to instead of writing about them.

I wouldn't claim that I receive more emails than anyone else but the constant stream of emails into my inbox has led me to devise some techniques for mini-mising the burden. My first strategy is treat your inbox like your Twitter feed – that is to say that if an important message is buried at the bottom of your inbox, it will likely come up again (probably by the sender resending it), so you don't need to stress out worrying that you might have missed something crucial. In my experience people who want an answer follow up after a while if they haven't received one.

Attend to internal emails, especially ones from higher ups, as a priority. They are usually easier to deal with as you can dispense with some of the pleasantries such as 'I hope you're well' (more on which later). For professional correspondence, using correct grammar and spelling is a good habit to get into. It helps to make the meaning of your emails clear to the sender. Keep all your emails as short and concise as possible.

Then deal with emails that are from people you know, and then from people you don't. I set aside some time in the morning when I first get into the office to deal with emails that came in overnight and ones that I didn't get to the day before. Then I do the same towards the end of the day – but not right at the end of the day. You don't want to become one of those people who only emails at 6 pm and expects an answer on the same day. I hate those people.

It's hard not to, but you shouldn't really bother with apologising that you have taken so long to respond to someone's email if it's only been a day or two. If it's been weeks then maybe some kind of brief explanation would be nice. We used to think email needed to be dealt with immediately when it was received because of the swift nature of the technology. I think we can all relax a little now and treat it like snail mail. You open it, you look at it, then you file it somewhere (either physically or mentally) and deal with it when you can.

I like to write my emails as though they are letters and use 'Dear X' as an opener and 'Kind regards' as a sign-off. I also put a space between my paragraphs and make an effort to spell things correctly, and use capital letters where necessary. But that's just me, and I do think it's acceptable to dispense with those niceties when you know someone or when you are emailing back and forth about a particular issue.

I used to have a boss who had no patience for long emails and would only read the first line, maybe two, of your email, which meant you needed to be succinct and to the point if you wanted an answer. It's a good habit to get into but it takes time to craft an email that is restricted to just one sentence. Don't bury the one question you need answered in paragraphs of text. I like to bold the one question I need answered so it stands out. Using all caps when you want something to stand out looks like you're shouting – bold is better. If you have a series of questions you need answers to then put them all together in the same part of the email and use bullet points to highlight them. Write your email in a series of paragraphs rather than one big paragraph. If I open an email and it's a wall of text then it's unlikely that I will read very far past the first line. And avoid using too many exclamation points. They're like swearwords – the more you use them, the less potency they have.

Some of the people I work with like to copy me in to nearly every email they send – or at least it sometimes seems that way to me. I've learned to ignore emails that I don't really need to read but I don't delete them in case there was something important in it. If you are copying people in to emails then you should only do it if it is important that they read this particular email or you have been instructed to do so. It's also a good tip to let the receipient of the email know that so-and-so is copied in. That will (hopefully) let them know to be careful what they write back if they hit reply all.

Sometimes you have had a long exchange of back and forth emails between colleagues and then need to forward that email, or at least some of it, to a third party. It's a good idea to go through the exchange and only forward what is absolutely necessary.

If you're sending something that is just an FYI or there is no need for the receiver to respond, then let them know that at the beginning of the email. It makes it easier for the person on the receiving end to manage their emails – they know they can just file this one for later. You can even put something like 'NNTR' (no need to respond) in the subject line.

If an email is urgent and requires a prompt response, then let the person you're emailing know by marking it as urgent in the subject line. But you should use 'urgent' sparingly. It's like crying wolf, the more you use it the less people believe you. The same goes with the use of 'confidential' – I occasionally receive emails (mostly from the same sender) that are marked 'confidential', and reading it becomes like a Where's Wally book. I spend my time searching for what on earth might be confidential in the contents of the email rather than what the sender is actually saying.

I sign off my emails in a variety of ways depending on who I'm emailing. 'Kind regards' is best if I don't know the person I am emailing and it's better to err on the side of formality. 'Regards' is also one I'm fond of if I know the person and am in a bit of a hurry, but signing off 'Kind regards' might seem overly formal and, therefore, robotic. 'Cheers' sounds a little too 'old boys' school' to me and I sometimes worry that the person I'm sending it to might be a teetotaller and will therefore take offence. 'Love' I reserve for friends only, even if I do have professional interactions with people that I love.

I also just use 'Best', even though some people don't like it as a sign-off. One of those people is the writer – and personal friend of mine – Nikki Gemmell. Writing in *The Australian* in June 2015, Gemmell said, 'Oh, I loathe that smarmy little word when it's rounding off an email. It's so perfunctory, cold, indifferent, curt.' As Gemmell noted, in the old days the rules were simple: '"Yours sincerely" if you'd actually met the person being written to; "Yours faithfully" if you hadn't. Few use those sentiments anymore – in fact, you'll be marked as a right old dinosaur if you do.' She is right on that front – I'm not sure how younger people might react to a sign-off like 'Yours faithfully'. I have even received the occasional email that was signed off 'KR' in place of 'Kind regards'. With email it's a case of horses for courses – you need to, as best as possible, without sounding like a fraud, adopt the writing style that your audience will be most receptive to. If I know someone well I often sign my emails just 'DM'.

How you begin an email is just as important. A lot of people – myself included – will open an email with 'Dear X, I hope you're well,' although it should be noted that I only do so when I actually know the person I'm emailing and genuinely do hope they are well. It's a convenient way of easing into your email, and, let's face it, most emails are about asking someone for something. So adding some padding before the ask makes you sound a lot less demanding. If 'I hope you're well' bothers you then try something a little more personal and specific. If you know the person is on the other side of the world and it's summer there, you could say something like 'I hope you're enjoying the summer, I hear it's been a hot one,' if you're the kind of person who needs a line between 'Dear X' and the real matter at hand.

Use the 'out of office' function (sometimes called a 'vacation reply') on your emails. It helps people to know your work situation – whether you're on holidays, away on business or have left the company – and gives them a sense of when they can expect a response to their email. I never use the out of office function when I'm just going to be busy or away from the office for a few hours as some people do. I think it sets up a false expectation that you will respond to their email as soon as you get back to the office, and we all know that's not true. When you set an out of office message, provide the email address of someone else who might be able to help the person emailing if you're going to be away for an extended period of time and not checking your emails.

Getting away from the office and planning not to be on email for any period of time requires a lot of advance preparation. You need to have meetings or catch-ups with people you deal with on a regular basis and let them know you will be away – that gives them the opportunity to get any business they might have coming up out of the way early. I make it clear in my out of office message if I won't be checking my emails and redirect to another member of my team. Then I give my team a back-up plan, part of which is that they should text me rather than email me if they urgently need to get in contact. That way I don't have to look at my emails at all and risk getting sucked into that never-ending vortex. You can do people a favour if you discover they are going to be away for a month after you send them an email, and that is to resend the email after they have returned to work rather than wait for them to go back through thousands of emails to get to it.

Most importantly, don't stress if someone doesn't respond to your email straight away. Send it again – but don't sound like a nag – they will most likely appreciate the gesture, as chances are they meant to get to your email but it slipped through the cracks. Don't waste time with emails that begin 'Sorry to bother you/ pester you' et cetera, because you're not sorry, you're just doing your job and following up, and it only makes the other person feel like they have failed in some way.

Finally, if something is super urgent then email is probably not the way to go – I'd opt for an old-fashioned telephone call or even a text message.

See also SENDING LARGE FILES VIA EMAIL.

EMAILS DURING MEETINGS

This also applies to text messaging and use of social media during meetings. Meetings run most quickly when everyone is paying attention and not wasting time with casual chit-chat, or being disruptive and speaking out of turn. I've sat in many meetings where one of the attendees has been texting or catching up on emails and then at a certain and crucial point in the meeting will say, 'Sorry, I missed that, can you go over that again?' Of course you missed it, your mind was on something else! If you're so busy that you have to email or text during a meeting or presentation, my advice would be to reschedule the meeting or send someone else in your place. Or just do what other people do and leave your correspondence until after the meeting.

If you're actually just taking notes on your phone or tablet device then it's a good idea to let the other people in the meeting know that's what you're doing – that way they won't think that you are not paying attention or have more important things you'd rather be doing.

EMOJIS

I love them and use them all the time, particularly when texting. In fact, when I send a text and I haven't used any emojis I look at it and think it lacks colour. Emojis are really just for fun but they can help to add or clarify the tone of your message. It's so easy when sending a short message to be misunderstood at the other end as curt, rude or in a bad mood. Adding an emoji or two helps to convey to the reader a little more information. They can speak volumes, but they are usually best used when you know the person you're messaging. After one or two messages between a new professional contact you can start using emojis if you think they are simpatico. After a while an emoji can take the place of any actual words in a text message or email, like a form of shorthand. They work particularly well on Twitter, where space is at a premium – just check out the Twitter feed of the Australian Minister for Foreign Affairs, Julie Bishop, if you want to see how they can be used effectively (twitter.com/JulieBishopMP). If you're the kind of person who gets offended when people use emojis in texts or emails then maybe you need to lighten up a little. Emojis in a formal letter or document, on the other hand, are best avoided unless you are writing to a cartoon character.

ENDING A CONVERSATION OR MEETING

There are some people who are great conversationalists but have a problem when it comes to ending a conversation – specifically they don't know how to, and that can make it awkward for the other person who realises the chat has reached its conclusion but now has to find a way to get out of it. There should be some way to make your phone ring with a fake call so you can excuse yourself and cease talking to the other person.

Until someone comes up with a way to do that there are a few other things you can do. I work with someone who just says 'great talk' when he's done as a way to get out of my office. It's not a bad move but it is the conversational equivalent of a heavy handshake – it can make you look a little dominating, especially if you're cutting the other person off. It's a little more polite to say something like, 'Is there anything else you'd like to discuss? If not, then that's all I have.' Then you can say your goodbyes and make an exit.

I have also worked with a boss who would either just stand up when she wanted the meeting to end or sometimes actually start walking out of her office to go about some other piece of business. It's a very effective way of letting someone know it's time to wrap it up but you have to be mindful of who you are doing it to. She was my boss and I would never have done it to her if she'd come to speak to me in my office. Mind you, she was also prone to saying things like, 'That's it, goodbye,' and remarkably no one in the office took offence at this – in fact she was admired for it.

If you have time constraints when someone comes to chat to you at work then be clear about it at the beginning of the conversation. If someone comes to my office and asks if I have a minute to chat about something, but I'm busy doing something or have to be somewhere, I will be blunt and say, 'Yes, but I have to do something in ten minutes.' Translated, that means 'Yes, but make it snappy.' If it's someone you know is always a chatterbox then it's advisable to state at the start of the conversation that you have to make a phone call/be somewhere in ten minutes, and then in ten minutes wrap up the conversation by motioning to make that phone call or head off to your appointment. When I do it but I don't actually have an appointment to attend, I just go to the bathroom or get a cup of coffee. I said I had an appointment in ten minutes, I didn't specify how long the appointment would be.

EXITING A BUILDING

When you walk out of a building, don't just charge into the footpath – look to see if someone is coming, as you would when getting out of a car. And don't crowd the entrance as there is possibly someone behind you who also wants to get out of the building, or someone who wants to get in.

If you're a smoker and the reason you are exiting the building is to have a cigarette, then wait until you are well out of the door before you light up and stand away from the door when you smoke. In some places the law dictates exactly how far away from the entrance to a public building or business you need to be if you are smoking – in New South Wales, for example, it's four metres, which personally I don't think is nearly far enough. No one wants to have to force their way through a crowd of people standing around shivering (why do smokers never seem to take a jacket with them when they go outside in winter?) and smoking just to enter a public building or business. And either dispose of your butts properly – which does not mean in the gutter outside the building – or take them with you.

See also REVOLVING DOORS.

F

FACEBOOK

In terms of social media, Facebook is old school. It was one of the first and as a result it's one of the biggest. Everyone is on Facebook. My eighty-something mother and my teenage nephews and nieces are on there. As are workmates past and present, friends I haven't seen in decades and people I see every day. My cleaner is on Facebook, as well as my local Thai takeaway. Having the vast majority of people you know following you on Facebook means you have to be extra careful about what you post. Remember, whatever you post might be read by your mother!

The first thing you should do is make sure you have your privacy settings watertight. You can choose what other people see regarding your Facebook activity and whether they can tag you in posts without your permission, among other things. The more control you have over these things the less likely other people's posts will cause offence to you and people you know. If you don't want your children to see a picture of you drunk to oblivion at someone's party then choose your settings accordingly. If you want people to be able to find you then use a recent and clear photograph for your profile picture. Remember that this photo is not just a profile photo – it also appears every time you post something or comment on someone else's post. Your employer, or potential employer, can also see your profile photo if they look for it, so G-rated is best here.

If you want to post photos you've taken of other people, it is polite to ask if it's okay first. Yes, you own the copyright to your photo but it's their image and they might not want certain photos of themselves to be publicly available. And if you are posting a photo of you with other people, make sure it's a good photo of everyone, not just you. It has taken me years to get a particular photo eliminated from cyberspace where everyone else looks fabulous but I have my eyes closed and look deranged. It would be nice to think that people will always ask before they tag you in a post but the reality is most times they won't. The best thing to do is configure your privacy settings so that you need to approve a post that you have been tagged in before it appears in your timeline. That way people can still post a photo of you but at least you won't be tagged if you don't want to be.

Interact and engage, like people's posts, comment and post something yourself occasionally. If you're deeply worried about your personal privacy then maybe social media isn't for you. Don't be a Facebook stalker, as it makes people feel like they're being watched. I always find it weird when someone says something to me in person about something I posted on Facebook, but they didn't like or comment on it online.

Keep it clean, remembering that anyone you know could be looking at it. If you want to be less censored in your posts (but still within Facebook's guidelines) then a good thing to do is set up a private group with some of your closest friends. It becomes kind of like a mini social network. I'm part of one that a friend set up several years ago and we use it as a forum to post things that we don't necessarily want all of Facebook to know about. It could be something as benign as one friend inviting everyone over for a swim in his pool on a hot day – it just saves him having to send out a bunch of text messages.

Consider changing your name. It's not as weird as it sounds. Unlike with Instagram or Twitter where you need an original username, on Facebook everyone with the name David Meagher can open an account under that name. Facebook is somewhere where potential employers and recruiters will look to see what a prospective candidate is like in a non-professional sense. This is another reason you should have your privacy settings set to Fort Knox–like security. As an alternative, though, there is nothing stopping you from changing your name to something else. Your friends will think it's odd when it first happens but they'll quickly forget about it. It just makes it harder for people who only know your name to find you, so you can comment on political and social issues and post photos of whatever you get up to on the weekend without any fear that someone who is considering you for a job will judge you based on what you do on Facebook. Or you can just keep your posts and comments squeaky clean under your real name.

Keep private conversations private – use Messenger rather than conducting a conversation with someone through posted comments.

Don't post obscene, crude or things of a sexual nature on someone's wall as it might be public and they might not appreciate that. Send it to them in a private message instead.

Don't argue or fight with someone online. If it becomes heated then take it offline or use Messenger instead.

Think before you comment, especially if it's a negative comment. Things can escalate on social media as people hide behind anonymity and can whip up a hate campaign in no time. If you think something *might* cause offence then you can rest assured that someone somewhere will find it offensive. Find a better way to say it, or don't say it at all. Remember you can be sued for defamation for comments and posts on social media.

Don't post or check in somewhere if you have taken a day off 'sick' from work.

Don't post drunk.

Don't post or check Facebook when you are driving.

If you're having a special event and you want it to be private then it's perfectly acceptable to ask your guests not to post things to social media. They will anyway, but at least you made your feelings clear. Or, if you think asking people not to post is going too far, perhaps ask them not to post on the night.

One of the great things about Facebook is that it reminds you about people's birthdays. I wish people a happy birthday on Facebook, but only if I know them well. People often bemoan that Facebook's birthday reminder has eliminated the need to send people a traditional birthday card. That might be true, but the Facebook function does allow you to wish many more people a happy birthday than you would normally send cards to. If someone is a close friend you could consider sending them a card – hard copy cards have taken on a greater level of intimacy now they are no longer essential – or send them a text, or pick up the phone and call them. If you don't want people to know when your birthday is, then turn off the function in your privacy settings. (A word of warning: the default privacy settings also let people know how old you are turning!) When you send someone a birthday message on Facebook it isn't private and it will appear on their timeline, so you should avoid mentioning how old the person is unless you're sure they're comfortable with everyone else on Facebook knowing that.

Can you ask to be friends with someone if you don't know them? Why not? A stranger is just a friend you haven't met before, and if you have friends in common then chances are you might like to know each other. It's also perfectly fine to send friend requests to people you've never met and have no connection to, but don't be too disappointed if your request is never accepted. There's a chance someone might think you're a fake account or a spammer if they have no friends in common with you. If you receive a friend request on Facebook from someone you don't know they should have at least one friend in common with you, which is how they have found you in the first place. Check out their timeline in order to work out if they are the sort of person you would want to follow, and if they have no posts or their account is private then it's probably best to ignore them.

Can you unfriend someone without causing offence? See UNFRIENDING SOMEONE.

When a person dies, their Facebook page lives on unless a spouse or family member goes through some rigmarole to shut it down. One of my friends died a few years ago after a long battle with cancer. She wasn't a particularly active person on Facebook but would post or comment or like something every now and then, and once a year I would be reminded of her birthday and wish her well. Now, several years after her passing, her friends still get a reminder of her birthday when it comes around. The first time it happened I found it incredibly sad, but now I love it. It reminds me of that person and I think of her each time I look at Facebook on that day. Whether or not someone's Facebook account should be cancelled after their death is up to those closest to the deceased. See also CONDOLENCE MESSAGES, PHOTOS AT A FUNERAL.

See also 'LIKING' (ON FACEBOOK, INSTAGRAM AND TWITTER).

FACETIME

See SKYPING IN PUBLIC PLACES.

FEET ON SEATS

It's somewhat baffling that this needs to be said, but feet don't go on seats, they go on the ground. Don't put your feet on seats on public transport, or in a cinema, or on a park bench. Seats are there for people to sit on, and if they wanted to sit on dirt and dog poo they would sit on the ground. If you exercise in a park don't use the benches in place of stair-climbing, use actual stairs, or something else that people don't have to sit on. If you do use the stairs, keep to one side so there's still room for other people to pass you.

FINGERNAILS

I'm going to sound like someone's mother here but your fingernails should always be clean and tidy. If you're a man and you hate cutting your fingernails, or if you're like me and your eyesight is bad and your left hand not as steady as your right, then consider getting a professional manicure every now and then. It's not emasculating and if you're worried about what people might think then just choose a manicurist who is not in the middle of a shopping mall or on a busy street. A manicure for men takes about twenty minutes, is not expensive, and is one less grooming ritual that you need to take care of at home. For women, if you paint your fingernails then they should be free of chips and scratches. The easiest and cleanest way to paint your fingernails is to have someone do them for you, which most people can't afford to do every week – but if you do paint your own nails, getting a manicure every couple of months will make your life easier because they will tidy your cuticles and nail beds, leaving clean, shaped nails for you to polish.

I have a colleague who paints her nails at her desk every Monday morning (she's always in the office early so she's finished before most people get in), which means her nails look fabulous for the working week. If you do your nails in the office it also means you have nail polish and remover handy if you need to do any touch ups during the week. Personally I quite like the smell of nail polish and remover, but some people don't, so be mindful of the people around you. Get in early like my colleague, or close your office door if you have one.

FOOD ALLERGIES

Food allergies, it seems, are so hot right now. Everyone has one and if you don't then you should get one. It's important to distinguish between a genuine food allergy – like coeliac disease – and just not liking the taste of coriander. Your aversion to coriander is not a food allergy and when you have accepted an invitation to dinner you don't have to say 'I don't eat coriander' unless a bite of it will send you to the hospital. You don't get to choose what you're eating at a dinner party – that's up to the host – and you have been invited into someone's home not just to be fed, but for your company and to contribute something to the social experience.

If you do have a genuine food allergy then you need to say so when you have accepted the invitation, not when you walk in the door. Similarly, if you order food in a restaurant then don't wait until the dish is placed in front of you to tell the waiter that you're allergic to nuts. Mention it to them when you are given the menu and they will be able to help you choose a suitable option. If your allergy is so dangerous that any food that has been prepared on the same surface or in the same kitchen as the ingredient you are allergic to will cause serious injury or death, then perhaps eating in a restaurant is not the most advisable thing to do.

When you tell someone about your food allergy, spare them the details of what will happen if you eat it, and refrain from making it the topic of conversation for the entire meal. I once sat next to a mother and her child on a one-and-a-half-hour flight to Melbourne. The flight attendant handed me a small bag of nuts and before I could open them the mother, who was seated next to me, reached for my hand and told me that her son is allergic to nuts and just opening the bag could cause him to breathe in nut particles. I said no problem, I didn't really want the nuts anyway. But then I had opened up the conversation and had to hear all about it, how serious it was, what would happen if he ingested even a fraction of a nut, and so on. I got the message, I complied with her request, and that should have been the end of it.

If you work with someone who is gluten intolerant and your workplace is the sort where it's common for someone to bring a cake to work when it's a co-worker's birthday, then try to find a gluten-free alternative so no one feels left out. Gluten-free cakes are pretty easy to make or purchase, and they can be just as delicious (mostly they substitute flour with almond meal). You don't need to make a big fuss about it as that will just embarrass the person who can't digest gluten – just let this person know that the cake you've brought in is gluten-free and they can make a decision as to whether they will indulge in a slice or not.

See also VEGETARIANISM AND VEGANISM.

FOOTPATHS

Most men of my age and older are probably aware that a man should always walk on the kerb side of a woman. When I was a teenager a female friend's father took me aside and told me he wanted to have a word with me. I thought, as most teenagers do, that it was going to be about either sex, drugs, smoking or all three. Instead what he told me was that when I'm with his daughter I should walk on the kerb side of the footpath. The origin of this tradition dates back to when streets were dirt roads and a passing horse and carriage could possibly splash dirt and mud onto pedestrians on the sidewalk. If a man walked on the outside then he would protect his female companion from getting dirty. It was also thought to protect women from being snatched by someone in a passing vehicle. This rule has pretty much gone the way of the horse and buggy, but there are some street rules which should never go out of fashion.

A busy footpath can be like a busy road so you should keep left to avoid constantly bumping into people. If people kept to the left it would make everyone's passage quicker as you wouldn't need to swerve out of an oncoming pedestrian's way.

Don't hug the building line when you walk as you might get hit by someone exiting a building. Be careful stepping out of a building and onto a busy footpath.

Don't hog the footpath. This is not the opening credits of *Sex and the City* so you don't need to walk four abreast.

For the life of me I don't know why adults need to hold hands on a busy footpath. If you do, then break apart if it's a narrow footpath and people are approaching, don't force them to dodge you.

Don't read a book or your phone while you walk.

Don't walk on someone's heels.

On a busy street be careful if you slow down to dawdle or window-shop. I once walked out of a shop on Madison Avenue in New York and, as I'm not from around there, I paused for a second to work out which way I needed to go. This part of New York is relatively genteel and not as busy as Midtown, but that didn't stop an elderly woman from yelling at me, 'Walk faster, this is New York, you know!'

See also CYCLING.

FORMAL WEAR

Every man, when he reaches adulthood and has settled into his particular body shape, should invest in a tuxedo or dinner suit. And when I say invest, I mean it. Don't buy a cheap dinner suit because you think you will only wear it once a year, if that. You should buy the best one you can afford. If you buy well and look after your dinner suit it will last you a lifetime. Buying well means you should also buy a style that is not too 'of the moment'. A classic, single-breasted, peak-lapel suit in black is all you need. I have one that I love and fully expect to keep wearing until I'm no longer invited to black-tie events. It's already about fifteen years old. Looking after it means having it cleaned from time to time, airing it out after you've worn it and before you hang it back in the wardrobe, and storing it on a quality cedar suit hanger in a suit bag (not a plastic one – find a cloth one, as plastic doesn't breathe and these bags can be a haven for mould).

These days the clothes suitable for formal occasions are as varied and creative as the dress codes specified on invitations. The following descriptions are the strict rules for what you should wear if an invitation calls for a certain dress code, taken from *Debrett's New Guide to Etiquette and Modern Manners*.

'White tie' or 'Evening dress': Usually reserved for very formal occasions and, thankfully, rarely seen these days. Men should wear a black evening tail coat, teamed with matching trousers with two lines of braid down the side, a stiff starched shirt, detachable stick-up or wing collar, a white bow tie, white waistcoat, black patent shoes with black ribbon laces and black silk socks. Women should wear a long, formal evening dress. Short dresses or trousers are not acceptable. You can see why white tie is rarely seen on invitations these days.

'Dinner jacket' or 'Black tie': For men this is what we think of as a traditional tuxedo. A man wears a black wool dinner jacket, which can be either single or double breasted, and should have ribbed silk lapels, no vents and covered buttons. Trousers should taper, be suitable for braces (that means no belt loops), and have one row of braid down the side. The shirt should be cotton or silk and either have a pleated or marcella front. It must have a soft turn-down collar, not the stiff winged variety, which strictly speaking is for white tie only. For women long or short dresses are fine, but long is more formal.

Meticulous formal wear is required increasingly infrequently. For most events a lounge suit is fine for men, which is basically the sort of suit you would wear to work, but preferably in a darker colour. If you're in doubt as to what the actual dress code is then try to ask the organiser or consult with some other people who you know will be attending.

In some respects women have it harder than men when it comes to formal wear (although the dress code for women at a black-tie event is a little more flexible). A woman can't really buy one dress and wear it to every black-tie event for the rest of her life, although there are women who more or less do that and always look chic. I once saw an exhibition at the Metropolitan Museum of Art in New York of the wardrobe of the style icon Countess Jacqueline de Ribes. One of the most fascinating things about this uber-stylish social-ite was that when she liked the design of a particular dress, which would often be by Yves Saint Laurent, she would ask the designer to make it for her in a few different colours. When she was onto a good thing she stuck to it. Buying a simple but elegant dress in a solid colour (people tend to remember having seen patterned dresses before more readily) will serve you well for many formal events.

FUNERALS

Like weddings, funerals today can take many different forms, and they won't always be conducted in a church. Unlike a wedding, however, a funeral is usually organised in a short period of time. If you've ever had to organise one, you'll know that there's a lot to do; and as a friend or family member you can help ease the burden by offering to help out. One of the easiest and most helpful things you can do is offer to let other people know when and where it will be.

The days of strict rules for funeral and mourning dress are long gone, but you should still make an effort to dress appropriately. The appropriateness of what to wear is determined not just by what kind of person the deceased was but also out of respect for their family and the type of ceremony. If it's a dawn memorial service on a beach, then clearly a suit and tie is not the most appropriate attire. You don't have to wear black to a funeral service but dark-coloured, unflashy clothes are best if it's a more traditional-style funeral. The day is not about you so you shouldn't dress to be the centre of attention. Women's jewellery should be inconspicuous and men should wear a jacket and tie.

Sometimes a funeral will have a specific dress code, such as wearing the deceased's favourite colour – you should make an effort to do this even if it's only with a small gesture such as a scarf or tie. You don't have to go head-to-toe canary yellow even if that was the person's signature colour.

If the family requests no flowers then you should adhere to that. Often it's because they don't want to have to deal with the business of finding vases for them and disposing of them after they have died.

On the day you should make an effort to help out without being asked. The organisers might not have had time to delegate some jobs such as seating people at the church or handing out food at the wake. If you see something that needs doing then just jump in and do it, no one will be upset about it.

See also PHOTOS AT A FUNERAL.

G

GAY AND LESBIAN

Is it okay to ask someone if they are gay? Ask yourself why you want to know first. If it's because you think someone is cute and you would like to ask them out on a date, and you are picking up a slight vibe then, yes, it's all right to ask them. If they're upset that you've asked them – for whatever reason – then the best thing to do is apologise profusely. If you're asking because you just want to know, then I would say it's none of your business and let people have some privacy. You might think it's no big deal – and it isn't – but some people like to keep some things about them private, and there are still some workplaces and social situations where being LGBTI might be an issue for other people.

GETTING A WAITER'S ATTENTION

A good waiter always has a sense of what the guests in the dining room are doing – where they are up to in their dining experience and how long they have had their meals in front of them. They are also adept at reading body language, and a good waiter will sense just by looking at you if you need their attention. A raised eyebrow or just eye contact should be enough. If that fails to get their attention then a raised finger should do it. A friend who has spent his entire working life in restaurants tells me that some people have more direct ways of getting his attention. Customers from some parts of Asia will just raise their hand like they are in a classroom and want to ask a question. It certainly works. Others will stand up and go and tap the waiter on the shoulder (no one, it should be said, ever responds well to being tapped on the shoulder), and others will just shout out. It's always good to remember that a waiter comes into contact with your food before you eat it, and wait staff have the power to make your dining experience a good one or a bad one. Try the discreet approach before getting out of your chair or yelling across the room. If all you're after is the bill then catching the waiter's eye and moving your hand like you are signing a cheque is the internationally accepted signal. Waiters don't find this rude and if it's a busy restaurant then they probably want you out quickly so they can seat someone else who is waiting for a table.

GOOD HOTEL GUESTS

I got a press release one day from an Australian hotel company that informed me the company was, and I'm paraphrasing here, turning the tables on its guests and asking its staff to review the guests. It was a response to customer reviews on sites like TripAdvisor, possibly a swathe of negative ones (I stayed at one of this company's hotels once and I have to say it wasn't a great experience). Nevertheless, I thought this was one of the dumbest things I'd ever heard. It was also clearly a desperate grab for some media attention. In the hotel business you only get press coverage when you have something new to say, and with no new hotels or renovations coming up they had to devise something else. It was a stunt to be sure.

What this gimmick highlighted, however, was that some guests behave appallingly when they stay in hotels. The idea behind the staff-review system was that if you got a good review you could possibly be upgraded or get some other benefit when you next stayed with the hotel group. My first thought was, is this really what a hotel has to do in order to get guests to behave properly? Remember when your mother would say something like 'This house is not a hotel', the implication being that she was not a chambermaid and would not be picking up after you, and, unlike a hotel, you couldn't just come and go as you pleased without any regard for the management and upkeep of the place? Well, a hotel is not your home, so that means you don't have to make your bed in the morning or pick up your towels from the bathroom floor. But that doesn't mean you can treat the place like a bordello. Make some effort to act like a respectable human being. Don't leave your room like a rock band has been staying in there, don't use the towels to clean your shoes (there's usually a shoe mitt for that) and don't steal things. If the housekeeping staff have done a great job at turning your pigsty back into a hotel room then you should leave them a tip, preferably each day, as it won't always be the same person cleaning your room. Just leave it somewhere obvious – the bed is as good a place as any – with a note that says thank you in the language of the country you are in. If you don't know how to say or spell it then download the Google Translate app to your phone; it's invaluable when travelling.

GRACIOUSNESS

Being gracious in defeat is one of the most admirable attributes a person can have. If someone gets a promotion that you wanted then no harm can come from sending them a message to say congratulations. If someone buys a bigger house and you're struggling to stay afloat in your shoebox apartment, or they buy a Maserati and you're still getting about in your clapped-out ten-year-old Mazda, then don't begrudge them their success. Tell them how excited you are for them and that you can't wait to see the house or go for a spin in the car. The result of your message can actually be more than being gracious. You'll look like a good sport and someone who behaves professionally – and that person who gets a leg up at work often has the ability to bring other people with them. And maybe that new house has a pool!

GRATUITIES

See TIPPING.

GROUP TEXTS AND MESSAGES

A group text or Facebook message can be a handy way of corralling a large group of people when you're trying to organise a gathering of some sort. They can, however, very quickly get out of control when someone decides to say something off topic, post a link to a funny video they've seen or keep butting in with irrelevant information. Group texts are like office meetings – you need to stay on topic for them to be useful. Complaining about how annoying this group message is will either make you look like a killjoy or will aggravate others into posting even more funny links and off-topic messages. It's also worth admitting that sometimes a consensus isn't going to be possible when organising an event, and maybe the best solution is to accept that not everyone can make it. If you are one of those people who knows you will be fine with whatever everyone else decides then let them know that you need to leave the conversation and you'll be cool with whatever the majority decides. Frankly, I think leaving is the best way to handle a rambling group message. If you use iMessage you can chose the 'Leave this conversation' option to exit a group text message. If it's a group message on Facebook Messenger then choose either 'mute conversation' or 'leave conversation' from the settings menu in the top right-hand corner of the message screen. Muting it is good as you can still go back at the end to see what the consensus was, you just won't be bothered with the constant new message notifications. It's for this reason that using Messenger or iMessage for organising social events is preferable to email as, depending on what email application you use, sometimes the only way to get out of a reply-all chain is to ask, and your request is almost never accepted.

GYMS

Most gyms and exercise studios have their own particular sets of rules for the behaviour of people who use them, but there are also some universal ones that should be observed to make working out that much more enjoyable for everyone.

Take a towel with you and wipe down the equipment after you have used it.

If you do yoga and you use one of the studio's mats, wipe it down after use.

Don't hog the machines. If someone is using the machine you want then ask if you can work in with their sets. If someone asks you then the only answer you can give is yes – you're in a shared facility. Don't drape a towel over a machine as a way to reserve it.

Put free weights back where they belong – leaving them on the floor is a safety hazard as well as inconsiderate to the next person who wants to use them.

Don't yell or grunt excessively when you're lifting weights. You don't sound tough doing it, you sound like a douchebag.

Don't pee in the shower.

If you do yoga you've probably been told at some stage that it's okay to break wind and is sometimes unavoidable. That's rubbish – it's always avoidable, or at least it should be. If you know you're a farter then take your position at the back of the room.

Don't take photos at the gym of anyone other than yourself.

H

HAND LUGGAGE

See OVERHEAD LOCKERS ON AEROPLANES.

HANDSHAKES

A good handshake is firm and brief. Remember what you're doing and concentrate on the act when you shake someone's hand. Sloppy handshakes are lazy handshakes. Avoid bone-crushing and limb-tearing handshakes unless you're trying to give the impression you have control issues. Stand up to shake someone's hand when they arrive at a dinner or a meeting table. If you can't get up, make a gesture towards standing when you shake their hand. Whenever someone says 'Don't get up' when they arrive at the table it's a bit like someone saying don't bring anything to a dinner party. Ignore them and get up. Kissing is a whole other subject, but basically should be avoided in professional settings unless you have a strong relationship with the person or you work in fashion, where kissing hello and goodbye is de rigueur. In any other professional situation, kissing as a greeting can smack of sexism.

HANGOVERS

Drinkers everywhere have myriad cures for hangovers, and whatever you've found to work for you is best (I go for fried food, aspirin and Coca-Cola). But the dull pain in your head is only half the problem: you need to convince others that you don't have a hangover at all. There is nothing worse than going to the office with a hangover and having everybody say things like, 'Well, when you go out mid-week . . .' all day long. The trick is to look good, or as good as you possibly can. Many people dress casually for work the morning after a big night out because they think it will make them more comfortable and therefore more productive on a day when the odds are stacked against them. Personally, I think this has the opposite effect – if you look bad you feel bad, and when you feel and look sloppy then it's going to be a very long day. So, on hungover days, a good trick is to dress up for work, make some extra effort when it comes to doing your hair, and shave even if you don't do it every day. It might sound silly, but it takes the attention away from the bags under your bloodshot eyes. And then if people say anything at all about your appearance that particular day then it will most likely be positive. Be sure to leave the office for lunch and eat a hamburger, and you'll power through the afternoon.

HATS

I've read (more than) my fair share of etiquette guides, and they all devote a lot of ink to the subject of wearing hats. No doubt it has something to do with the era in which they were first published. At the turn of the twentieth century all adults wore hats when outside the house, and the tradition continued into the 1950s (we've all seen *Mad Men*). There were different rules for men and women, and for men it was important to know when you should tip your hat (or raise it just slightly off your head for a moment) and when to take it off completely. For example, a man would always take off his hat when in the presence of a woman or when indoors. Women, on the other hand, were permitted to keep their hats on, presumably as removing them would leave them with unsightly hat hair. The exception to this rule was a woman who was attending the theatre and wearing a hat that might obstruct the view of the person behind them.

Today hats are worn as either a fashion item or for protection from the sun. I don't think it's too much of a throwback to expect people to remove their hat when indoors unless religious customs dictate that they keep it on, or if your hair is going to look so terrible it would be easier to leave the hat where it is. Men should never wear a hat at a dinner table unless it's outdoors and you need protection from the sun. If you're wearing a hat with a wide brim then be mindful of your increased head circumference. You also need to pay particular attention to your hat when you kiss someone hello or goodbye. Tilting your head sideways is helpful.

HOLDING THE DOOR OPEN

Maybe I'm just old fashioned, but when I go through a door I look behind me and hold it open if there is someone on my tail. I expect them to say thank you, or nod or smile in acknowledgement, and for the most part they do. Because of this, I get really annoyed when someone doesn't show me the same courtesy. If you're capable of opening a door for yourself then you're capable of holding it open for someone just behind you, or someone exiting the building just after you have entered. If someone doesn't hold a door open for me when it's pretty obvious it would have been no big deal for them to do so I make a point of saying 'Thank you' anyway. I've always been ready with a witty one-liner for when the person asks why I thanked them but the thing is, they never do. People who open a door and charge through it with no regard for anyone else are usually oblivious to what is going on around them. Once I said thank you to a man who entered a shop just as I was leaving but refused to hold the door for that extra split second so I could grab it, and he said, 'I'm holding a baby, you idiot.' Well, he wasn't holding the baby with both hands and was able to open the inward-swinging door for himself, so handing the open door to me wouldn't have caused him to drop the baby. But what goes around comes around. If you want to live in a civil society where people hold the doors open for other people, where people offer an elderly, frail or pregnant person their seat on public transport, or where people just generally look out for others, then you should lead by example and hold that door open for someone.

HOSPITAL WAITING ROOMS

People find themselves in hospital waiting rooms on all sorts of occasions – some happy and some not so happy. For that reason, it's a good idea to keep them as peaceful as possible. It's also highly likely that you could be waiting for a long period of time. If you take children with you to the hospital then pack something to quietly amuse them. If they are playing with a mobile device, make sure they wear headphones. Mobile technology has changed the nature of childhood boredom and should be embraced by parents for the sake of other people. Many hospitals will have rules about mobile phones – whether or not they should be switched to silent or whether calls are permitted – and about bringing in outside food. Obey the rules for the sake of others – patients, visitors and staff. Respecting other people's need for quiet can make a stressful and upsetting wait just that little bit easier to bear.

HOST OR HOSTESS GIFTS

I know the word 'hostess' sounds sexist and like something straight out of the 1950s, but I couldn't come up with a better word. If you're invited to someone's house for dinner or a party then it's nice to take a small token of your appreciation of the effort they have gone to. They have probably been shopping, cooking and cleaning all day, and all you had to do was get dressed and show up. As well as taking a bottle of wine – that's a given – you should take something else as well. It doesn't need to be big or extravagant; in fact it shouldn't be, as you don't want to embarrass the host or the other guests. Something perishable like food – chocolate, biscuits et cetera – or a small bunch of flowers (big bunches can be a pain for the host to accommodate, and if you do take flowers, make sure to help out with the arranging if the host is busy cooking), or a scented candle is always nice. At Christmas time when you are invited to a lot of parties, prepare in advance and have some gifts ready to go. This is a situation where your regifting cupboard might come in very handy. See REGIFTING.

HOUSE GUESTS

While your home is not a five-star hotel, you should make every attempt to ensure house guests have a comfortable stay. After all, you may want to stay with them some day. The trick is not to make it so comfortable they overstay their welcome or never leave. As a benchmark, a week is the maximum stay, unless someone is a very close friend or a relative – or unless you stayed at their place for three weeks in the past. Like many issues around what's good and bad manners, when it comes to close friends and family rules are not necessary, and hospitality in particular should come with no strings attached.

To make guests feel at home, be there to greet them when they arrive. Finding a key under a rock in the garden is okay if you know the house you're visiting, but can be more like an obstacle course if you've never been there. Give your guests their own key for the duration of their stay so they don't have to come and go when you do.

Provide comfortable bedding, including clean pillows and fresh towels, and leave spare blankets in their room in case they are needed. If your guests are arriving at night after a long journey, have the bed made up so they can crash. Provide somewhere for them to hang a few clothes, and show them how to use your washing machine and dryer, if you have them and your guest is staying for more than a few days. Laundry takes on great significance when you've been travelling for a while. If you live in an apartment building, let them know about any body-corporate rules that might affect them, such as whether it is permissable to hang washing on the balcony.

I've had some fantastic experiences as the house guest of friends living in foreign cities, which have made my experience of visiting that country all the more fulfilling. And it's the small things that make a huge difference. Guidebooks and maps beside the bed, a weekly train ticket for my stay, a list of my host's various telephone numbers, my host's address printed onto a business card in the native language of the country (very handy for getting a taxi home if you don't speak the language), a printout of the wi-fi password, to name just a few things that have been godsends when staying in a strange city.

If you are a guest in someone's house, don't overstay your welcome, and make sure you give your hosts a gift at the end of your stay. The gift doesn't need to be extravagant, and by giving it at the end of your stay you give yourself some time to figure out what they might appreciate or need. You should also make an effort to fill the fridge from time to time, just for the heck of it, and replace anything that you break during your stay, like a wineglass. Remember it's not a hotel, and be on your best behaviour – you don't want to become someone's dinner-party horror story for years to come. There's also no housekeeper coming in to clean the room after you leave, so tidy up after yourself and put the sheets and towels you used in the washing machine.

I

IN-FLIGHT ENTERTAINMENT

Most airlines offer a wide variety of entertainment these days in all cabin classes. I guess they have figured out that keeping passengers entertained with a range of options prevents them from getting bored and becoming unruly. Despite this, many people, myself included, download their own selection of movies and television shows to watch while travelling. I only say what I'm about to say because I have actually seen it happen: don't watch pornography on a plane, unless you are in a first-class suite and no one else can see your screen, but even then this is probably not the place to do it.

You should also be mindful of who else can see your screen, even for non-X-rated viewing. You might be sitting next to or across the aisle from a young child or someone who may find your choice of entertainment offensive. If you're watching a hilarious comedy after the lights have gone down then please remember that the rest of the cabin might be sleeping, and someone laughing at the top of their lungs, while extremely amusing the first time it happens, gets tiresome when you're trying to read or sleep. Always use headphones when watching a movie on your computer or mobile device in a public place, planes included.

INSTAGRAM

Instagram is an image-sharing social media platform, so think about the visual quality of the image you want to post. Is it really Instagram-worthy? Or is it something that might be better suited to another service, like Twitter or Facebook, where there is less emphasis on aesthetics? Most people look at Instagram on a mobile device, which means when they view your image it will be relatively small. Although Instagram has recently added the ability to zoom in on a photo, it's still a good idea to post an image that can be viewed easily on a mobile phone screen without needing to zoom. Instagram doesn't seem to be a platform for deep contemplation so if you don't grab someone's attention quickly and clearly then they will just scroll down to the next image.

If your aim is to get more followers then people will be more likely to follow you if you mostly post quality images – that means they should be in focus and nicely composed. There is a certain well-known fashion editor who posts endless images from fashion shows on her account and they are mostly out of focus. I realise not everything needs to be pin–sharp and it can be difficult to capture a moving target in focus, but when your caption reads 'Just take a look at the incredible embroidery on this jacket', then it's safe to assume the person who is posting the image intended it to be clear and in focus. I have looked at this person's Instagram feed and wondered if she might need a new prescription for her glasses. This particular Instagram-mer also posts way too many pics, and if they were great images people wouldn't mind, but when you open your Instagram feed and it's full of crap photos all from the same person then chances are that person will lose followers.

In the past Instagram showed you posts from accounts you followed in chronological order, but today it uses an algorithm to determine what to show you based on other posts you have engaged with (that is, liked or commented on). So, if you want to build up your following on Instagram, you need to post images that people are more likely to engage with. Using hashtags when you post a photo is another way to attract more followers, as other users might click on a hashtag to see what other people have posted using that tag, and they might find your photo and profile and like what they see.

Instagram has rules about what kind of images you can share, and if you break those rules they will remove your post. If you keep doing it you will find yourself banned from the network. That's a good thing, and I don't say that because I don't like nudity (I do), but it seems that if a picture sharing service is unregulated then it very quickly becomes just another repository for pornography, and that can get boring – just look at Tumblr if you don't believe me. That doesn't mean you shouldn't think about the appropriateness of the image you want to post.

If the company you work for has guidelines around using social media at work then you should acquaint yourself with them before you post images taken in your workplace or comment on other people's images.

How much is too much? Instead of posting ten photos of your fabulous day at the beach, maybe just post the best two or three and make sure they are markedly different from each other. Instagram is great for sharing shots from your holiday and, for the most part, people like opening the app on their phone and seeing nice shots from faraway places. Over-sharing, however, can turn you from a humble holiday-maker into a smug bragger. Three photos a day when you're travelling seems to hit just the right balance. There are no hard and fast rules about how much to post, and if your images are great then people will no doubt want to look at lots of them, but if you're travelling with a friend or a group of friends, or attending the same event, there is a high probability that you will share a lot of the same followers on social media, so if all of you are posting a dozen images a day that can clog a person's Instagram feed and become annoying. Another good reason to limit yourself to a handful of posts per day.

Endless selfies are pretty boring for the viewer, mainly because they are always taken from the same angle and distance. I put selfies in the same category as watching The Real Housewives of Wherever – it's fun to do every now and then but too much of it makes you want to throw something at the screen in disgust at the pure narcissism on display. If your aim is to build up your followers on Instagram then you should offer people more than just hundreds of photos of your face. Mix it up a little.

If you take a photo of someone or a group of people always ask if they mind if you post it to Instagram.

Don't steal other people's images. If you regram something then credit the original poster. And wait a little while before you regram it, if it's likely that you share many of the same followers. They won't want to see the same image twice in the space of a few minutes.

A picture is supposed to say a thousand words, so keep your photo captions brief. People follow you on Instagram because they like the images you post, not to read five-hundred-word musings on the photo you posted. Hashtags can help add further explanation to your photos but making up long and indecipherable ones that require someone to stop and stare at it until they can work it out are #justmakingyoulooklikeacompleteidiot.

Personally I hate graphically designed inspirational quotes posted as images on Instagram – they seem like something better suited to Twitter, if they are suited to any medium at all. Or maybe you could make a needlepoint cushion out of them? Either way, I'd be very happy if people could just stop the quotes. Typesetting a quote nicely doesn't make it any truer. And speaking of truth, if you do post quotes from people, make sure they are correct and properly attributed.

Liking your own images is weird and unnecessary. We know you liked it, the fact that you posted it to Instagram tells us so.

Unless your aim is to be a cyberbully then you should contain your comments on Instagram to the benignly positive. There are times when you look at someone's post and you really want to call them out for being a twat, but exercising restraint is the best course of action in these cases. I realise it's hard sometimes, but just keep scrolling and move along to another image, and the urge will pass. If you are on the receiving end of a negative comment the best way to handle it is to rise above it and ignore it. If it's offensive then you can delete it from your post by opening up a new comment on the image and then swiping left on the offending comment rather than starting an all-out cyber war in retaliation.

And remember, some things should remain private, like going to the dentist. You can document every aspect of your life if you want but you don't really need to share that picture of you in the dentist's chair with your mouth wide open.

See also 'LIKING' (ON FACEBOOK, INSTAGRAM AND TWITTER), SELFIES AND SELFIE STICKS.

INTRODUCTIONS

In 1922 the American writer Emily Post wrote what would become one of the all-time bestselling books on etiquette. *Etiquette in Society, in Business, in Politics and at Home* has been updated several times over the ensuing decades and is still in print today. When Post first wrote her book the most common etiquette mistakes people made, she said, apart from which piece of cutlery to use, involved introductions. The whole palaver of who gets introduced to whom revolved around issues of prominence and was overlaid with a good dollop of sexism.

Strictly speaking, the proper order of introduction is that the less prominent person is introduced to the more prominent person, the younger person is introduced to the older person, and a man is always introduced to a woman. (See what I mean?) But what happens when two women of roughly the same age need to be introduced? 'In making introductions between ladies whose social ranks differ,' wrote Noreen Routledge in 1944, 'the lady of lower rank is always introduced to the one of higher rank, even though the former may be an older woman, or married.' Nowadays, the whole notion of prominence has pretty much been dispensed with. I think the only women who hold on to the concept of rank today are the fictional ones on *Downton Abbey*.

Post, it should be remembered, was an American, and her writings on etiquette, while incredibly thorough, were rooted in an attempt to emulate the conduct of the British upper class. Today introductions can be done in any order so long as you exercise a little common sense. You should always give people's full names. 'Joe, this is Mary, Mary, this is Joe,' is not enough, especially in a business setting. You should always use last names, including when you're introducing yourself.

Post also recommended that you give some background information as well. 'I'd like you to meet my husband John' (or John Smith if your last name is different to your husband's). Substitute husband for colleague, friend, personal trainer or whatever the case may be. You can also add in some other information such as 'Joe Smith, this is Mary White. Mary's also a microbiologist.' Giving context helps the people being introduced to remember one another's names, as they have something to associate it to. Try to speak slowly and clearly when you're introducing someone to give people a chance to hear it. How many times have you been introduced to someone and had no idea what the person doing the introductions said?

There is no need to use titles such as Mr, Mrs, Miss or Ms in introductions. Other titles, such as Professor, Doctor, General, et cetera, may be necessary in certain professional situations, but socially they come across as pretentious.

Don't wait for an introduction if it doesn't appear to be forthcoming. And unless you are hobnobbing with royalty don't worry about issues of prominence, age or gender either. If you are going to meet someone from a royal family you will be informed by their protocol office about the correct way to handle the introduction.

When you do introduce yourself, just come out with it clearly. Say 'I'm John Smith' and stick out your hand to shake. It's also not a bad idea to add in some other information, such as 'I'm John Smith, I'm a colleague of Michael's,' that is, if Michael is your host. If you are introducing someone to your boss, then you may want to follow the sequence of less prominence introduced to more prominence to show due respect.

'Pleased to meet you,' is actually considered to be an English lower class way of responding to an intro-duction. The upper classes would respond by repeating the greeting. In other words, 'How do you do?' 'How do you do.' Saying 'How do you do?' is a good habit to get into. It doesn't really matter what the other person says – it might be 'Hi' or 'Howdy' or 'G'Day' – but responding with 'How do you do?' is a good all-purpose response. It might smack of rah-rah English toffs, but at least it's easy to remember. You should never answer a 'How do you do?' with a 'Quite well, thanks,' or, worse, 'I've got a bit of a cough, actually,' and then stick out your hand. Keep it simple. 'Hello' is all you really need to say. You could, however, add in an 'I've heard so much about you.' Under no circumstances should you say 'Charmed', 'Delighted' or 'Enchanted' unless you're a drag queen.

If you are taking a guest to a function where you know most of the people and they don't, you don't need to drag them around the room and introduce them to everyone in attendance. Introduce them to people as you encounter them in the natural course of the function, and don't abandon them until they have met enough people in order to survive the event on their own.

Don't leave someone hanging. If someone approaches you and you can't remember their name and you've only met them once before then just be honest and say something like, 'I'm so sorry, I have completely forgotten your name,' and then go ahead with the introductions and try not to forget it again. If, on the other hand, you've met this person several times before then you're in a spot of trouble. If the moment allows you can ask the person you are with to jump in and introduce themselves because you've forgotten the name of the person approaching. If your guest is perceptive they might be able to read the body language between you and the person to be introduced and jump in to save the day. But if that doesn't work then about the only other thing you can do is quickly ask 'Have you two met before?' and hope that they introduce each other. That is your opportunity to listen and learn, and again, try not to forget that person's name next time.

Remembering someone's name is a great skill and always makes the other person feel good. One way to attempt to do it is to repeat the person's name back after you have been introduced. 'John, how do you do?' Even saying it to yourself will help to plant something in your memory. If someone has a difficult last name to pronounce then ask them to say it again and repeat it back. As someone who has a difficult last name to pronounce I'm always pleased when someone wants to make an effort to say it properly. Then if you want you can ask them about the significance or origin of their name and you will probably never forget it.

If you're the host or the organiser of a business meeting or a small gathering of friends who might not have all met one another before then, when everyone has arrived, even if some of the guests have spent some time chatting among themselves, it's a good idea to begin the proceedings by asking if everyone knows each other or has been introduced. If not then do it there and then by going around the table – even if it is doubling up on some introductions, it can be a good way to break the ice.

J

JOGGING

I run, and I choose to do it early in the morning. I run at that hour for the solitude and for the simple fact that there is little chance anyone I know will see me, as I am not the most graceful runner. People who run usually do so on a footpath and, as we have discussed earlier, footpaths are for sharing. When you run on a footpath you have to keep an eye on potholes and fallen tree branches, pedestrians, cyclists and dogs, and weave between them all. If you're moving faster than the average walker then it's probably easier for you to duck and weave around them rather than to expect them to get out of your way. As a runner, I know that when you're in the zone it's much easier to navigate your way around obstacles based on intuition rather than a set of rules. However, if a pedestrian does get out of your path as you're running towards them then a small wave of thanks wouldn't go astray.

If you see a friend when they are running please don't be offended that they didn't stop to chat. It's not the Olympics but, all the same, we have a heart rate to maintain.

If you like to run with a group then be mindful that other people are using the footpath and don't be overbearing. A group of runners coming at you can be intimidating for a pedestrian out for a leisurely stroll.

JUMPING THE QUEUE

See QUEUE JUMPING.

K

KEEP YOUR DISTANCE

I'm not neurotic – really, I'm not – but I get uneasy when someone walks close behind me. I don't like it because, first, it's an invasion of my personal space and, second, it's an aggressive move that makes the person in front of you feel like they have to walk faster or they will be run into. It's the pedestrian equivalent of tail-gating someone when you're driving (when I learned to drive I was taught that if you couldn't see the tyres on the car in front of you then you were too close). In some cities – I'm thinking London, New York and Shanghai just to name three – it's almost impossible to walk down a street and not have someone hot on your heels. But in most places it is possible to walk and leave a comfortable gap between you and the person in front of you. If the person in front of you is walking too slowly then speed up and overtake them. I think one of the reasons that people seem to be walking too close to others more is that people often wear headphones while they're walking, and headphones give you a distorted perception of personal space. They create a world that blocks out the outside sound. It makes you feel like you're separate from what is going on around you – and to be fair, the reason for wearing them sometimes is to separate yourself from the world – which means you forget about keeping your distance.

Public transport is another place where you don't want people standing too close to you. Sometimes it's unavoidable – such as on a crowded train or bus – but you should be mindful of other's people's personal space. Just a few centimetres would be nice. When you're in a crowded situation such as a peak-hour train or bus, then try to avoid the temptation to read over the shoulder of the person in front of you – that just makes an already uncomfortable situation creepy.

Sometimes close talking is essential if you want to make yourself heard – for example, at a nightclub or bar, or in a noisy restaurant – but when it comes to everyday conversations you should keep a respectful distance. The space it takes to reach out and shake someone's hand is a good guide. If you can smell what the other person ate for lunch on their breath, then you're too close.

Don't stand too close to people in queues; it doesn't make the queue move any faster and feeling someone breathe on the back of your neck certainly doesn't make it any more pleasant.

KINDNESS

What's the difference between manners and etiquette, you ask? Etiquette, being the French word for 'label' or 'ticket', has its origins in the French royal courts of the seventeenth and eighteenth centuries. It was a daily list of events that not only recorded the time and place for the event but also the proper dress for each. It was a set of hard and fast rules, and breaking them was social taboo. You didn't have to think about why you should behave in a specific way for a particular place and time, you just had to follow the rules. Etiquette is an infrequently used term these days, not just because it's old-fashioned and rooted in snobbery but because no one likes being told what to do.

Manners, on the other hand, are open to interpretation. Manners are an acknowledgement that there is more than one way to behave in a particular situation, but the underlying element that defines what 'good' manners are is kindness. Good manners is putting yourself in someone else's shoes. How would you feel if you were stuck at an intersection trying to get into a queue of traffic when you're trying to get somewhere on time and no one will let you in? You know that will be you one day, so be the driver who shows some kindness to another driver. The 'rules' in this case are road rules, which, strictly speaking, say nothing about letting someone into a queue of traffic. So the driver in the traffic is not breaking any laws by staring ahead and ignoring the person trying to get in, they're just being unnecessarily mean.

I don't normally go in for karma and all that stuff, but, as I said in the introduction to this book, just as other people's bad behaviour can bring out the worst in people, so too can good behaviour bring out the best. Be kind, open a door for someone, let someone jump ahead of you in a queue, help someone lift their luggage off of a baggage carousel – if they are a decent human being they might reciprocate the gesture to you or pay it forward to someone else.

L

LATENESS

A friend – someone who I had not known for very long – once said to me, 'Are you always so punctual?' I was due to meet him at his house at 7 pm one night and if memory serves me I probably rang the doorbell right on the stroke of seven. I was also probably outside his house, walking around the block or sitting in my car waiting for it to actually strike seven. The way he said it suggested he found punctuality to be a character flaw, like when someone asks, 'Are you always this perky in the morning?'

After writing my 2005 book on manners I was frequently asked by people what was the one act of bad manners that really annoyed me. I didn't have to think about it. Lateness. 'Oh, but I always text people when I'm running late,' someone would invariably say. Well, that might seem like politeness, but it doesn't really help the person who bothered to turn up at the appointed time when he gets a message at ten past the hour that you are a few minutes away. All it does is keep the person informed – they don't get that time back. Just don't be late in the first place. Many years ago I stopped being friends with someone on account of her chronic lateness. I saw her lateness as an act of selfishness and, to me at least, it felt like she had no regard for my time.

My doctor, who I have been seeing for about twenty years, always seems to be running late and to compensate for this I always try to get an early morning appointment – the logic being that he will be far less likely to be running behind schedule at 8.30 am. A few months ago I needed to see my GP to get a referral to another doctor. I made a 9.15 am appointment as it was the earliest he had but I didn't get to see him until 10.20 am. That's more than an hour! I was livid and when I did finally see him I let him know. I explained that his time was no more valuable than mine and that if I make an effort to be here on time (I was actually there at 9 am) then he should make an effort to see me on time as well, or at least let me know how late he is running so I can go and do something else. He's never kept me waiting since. When I went to see the doctor I was being referred to I read the referral on his computer screen (I wasn't snooping – he was showing me something on the screen) and I noticed that my GP had written 'Patient can be irritable.' I let the specialist know that, yes, patient can indeed be irritable when patient is kept waiting for over an hour.

You can fix chronic lateness, however. I once interviewed the CEO of a major company and I happened to see his electronic diary on his laptop. I noticed that before and after his appointments he had inserted 'travel time' so that he didn't end up with back-to-back meetings. I asked him about it and he said it was his personal assistant's doing as he used to always run late for appointments. When I asked if the strategy was working he said that he was not perfect but was getting there.

My response to my friend who asked if I was always so punctual was 'I certainly am, and if I'm ever late you should call the police because something has probably happened to me!' I once made an arrangement to visit a friend at his house and we agreed on 'around 6 pm' as the rendezvous time. He lives in an inner-city suburb and I was having trouble finding a parking spot so by the time I got to his place it was approaching 6.10 pm. When he answered the door he looked like someone had just died. 'What happened?' he asked. I told him I couldn't find anywhere to park and he said that he and his partner were starting to worry because I'm never late. I took that response, and his concern, as a compliment.

Being on time actually means being a few minutes early. If a meeting is scheduled for 10 am, you should be in the room ready to go at 9.55 am. You should know how long it will take you to get somewhere, work out how you will get there, and add a few minutes for good measure. If you use Google Maps to plan your trip it will give you an estimated travel time for various forms of transport, making it easy to plan ahead. Being late means you are wasting other people's time. Texting to say you are running a little late should not be a fallback.

If I book a table at a restaurant then I will show up a few minutes before the appointed time. I'm not one of those people who needs a reminder about a restaurant booking or a dental appointment. Ralph Lauren's restaurant in New York City, the Polo Bar, is one of the most difficult restaurants in the city in which to secure a reservation – it's almost like a military manoeuvre. There's even a dress code. But when you do finally get a reservation you get a call on the day before to check that you're still coming and a warning that if you are more than fifteen minutes late then your table might be given away. Frankly, I think fifteen minutes is overly generous.

A lot of being well-mannered is just about not being an arsehole. Don't text someone to say you're running late when it's already five minutes past the appointed time. It's only wasting that person's time. I could do something with that extra fifteen minutes if I know in advance.

Then there are the time negotiations. If we have a

breakfast meeting at, say, 8.30 am, where the time was agreed upon many days earlier, then turn up on time. Don't send me a message the day before and say could we make it 8.45 am and then on the day of the meeting text me at 8.45 am to say you're running ten minutes late. That means the 8.30 am meeting is suddenly a 9 am meeting, which is not what I wanted, or I would have suggested that time when we first planned the meeting.

The best way to become a more punctual person is to manage your diary better. Don't overcommit, factor in how long it will take you to get to each appointment and don't say yes to things that you know are unrealistic, like agreeing to an 8 am meeting when you know you will never get yourself out of bed to be there in time.

LEAF BLOWERS

I live on a busy street within a densely populated suburb of Sydney and, frankly, if the only sound I had to annoy me was a leaf blower then I'd be extremely happy. Besides, leaf blowers conjure images of suburban streets with perfectly manicured gardens, and where I live is far removed from that. A couple of years ago, however, my neighbour across the street gave his boyfriend a leaf blower for Christmas. An odd choice for a Christmas gift, I know. I was unaware of this snazzy new gadget until autumn came and the leaves started gathering on the ground. Our street is lined with plane trees and when the weather turns the leaves drop like nobody's business. Removing them from our street would be like painting the Sydney Harbour Bridge – once you finished it would be time to start again. Which is exactly how it felt that autumn. I thought he would tire of it but he didn't. On Good Friday of that year, a day when hardly anyone works and most services are not operating, I was woken to the sound of a leaf blower that just didn't stop. I'd had enough so I sent the person who gifted this leaf blower a message on Facebook. 'Your boyfriend really likes that leaf blower,' was all I said. Like magic, the leaf blower stopped and I heard the sound of a door slamming. Sometime later I had a discussion in the park about the incident with the person responsible for giving the leaf blower – I felt bad that I asked him to stop the noise in such a curt manner – and he said it had become a huge problem and his partner just wouldn't stop using it, and all the neighbours had complained, not just me. I suggested he buy him a really nice broom instead. And now all we hear is the soothing sound of sweeping.

There are no laws governing the use of leaf blowers and from what I can gather it must be a very comforting thing to use, so tread carefully when you bring up the noise it makes with your neighbour. It might seem cowardly but sometimes I think a note in the letter-box might do the trick and avoid a potentially nasty confrontation.

'LIKING' (ON FACEBOOK, INSTAGRAM AND TWITTER)

You need to like in order to get likes – that's how people find you. You like a photo on Instagram, one of that poster's followers clicks on your name to see what your profile is like and, if they like what they see, you get a new follower. That doesn't mean that you should like every single thing you see, that just makes you look like a stalker and, let's face it, not everything your friends post is that likeable. Having said that, it doesn't cost anything and only involves the click of a button or a double tap on an image to like something, and in doing so you will make the person who posted it feel pleased with themselves. You can also get new followers by using hashtags to categorise your post. You shouldn't hashtag your posts to death, either; it just ends up looking like a wall of meaningless text. If your goal is to attract more followers, then use hashtags that are not overly obvious. If you use something like #fashion then there will be millions of posts with that hashtag and the chances of someone finding yours are slim.

Be aware that liking can have different connotations depending on your social network. On Instagram it just means you like what you see and on Twitter it means you agree with the sentiment expressed in the tweet or link. On Facebook, however, it could mean that you are expressing your sympathy with someone who has just lost a loved one, or you're happy that someone just had a birthday, or you're cranky that a tree is about to be knocked down in your neighbourhood. Even though Facebook recently moved from just having a like button to also having 'Love', 'Haha', 'Wow', 'Sad', and 'Angry' buttons, the default action is to 'Like' something, and that's what people seem to be sticking with. Liking a post about someone whose cat has died doesn't mean that you like the fact that their cat is dead but that you feel their pain.

If you think your 'like' on Facebook or Instagram might be misinterpreted then leave a comment instead, or reply, retweet or quote the tweet on Twitter. It's important to remember that other people can see what you've liked or commented on, and social media networks tailor their advertising to you based on your activity – such as liking – on their network. You do something seemingly innocent one day, such as liking a link someone posted to a story about how bald men are sexier, and for the next two weeks you are subjected to advertising from hair replacement companies.

LINKEDIN

LinkedIn is a valuable networking tool in some industries, less so in others. Unlike Facebook, where it is more or less a given that you will have some sort of personal connection to a person before you ask to be their friend, LinkedIn is for professional networking, so it is perfectly acceptable to ask to link in with someone you don't know if they are in a related field and, on face value at least, there might be a mutually beneficial reason for the two of you to connect.

LinkedIn is also a tool that is used by recruiters and employers not only to find suitable candidates but also to check the credentials of a candidate they are already considering. For that reason you should keep your LinkedIn profile clean and professional. A photo of you at the beach without a shirt on and a drink in your hand is not appropriate for LinkedIn – that's better for Facebook (although see that entry earlier for issues around profile pictures on Facebook). The same goes for the sorts of articles you share on LinkedIn – keep them relevant to your industry and profession.

LinkedIn has very good search engine optimisation, which means when a potential employer does a Google search of your name it's likely your profile will be one of the top three returned search items. You should therefore make an effort to keep the information up to date and informative. LinkedIn has replaced the need for a hard-copy resume and a potential employer may read your LinkedIn profile before they make contact with you, so populate it with a bit more than job titles and dates. And don't fabricate any of the information, as it is so much easier for a potential employer to verify things today than it was before the internet, and they will do it without you knowing, which means you won't get an interview and therefore an opportunity to impress someone with your charm.

LITTERING

Apart from being illegal in most places and having health implications, it's also just lazy and rude. It shows a complete disregard for civility. I don't really care if your house is a pigsty but outside your house I expect people to live like human beings and not animals.

I take littering seriously. I once drove into the carpark at work behind a colleague who threw his cigarette butt out the window as he turned off the street and into the driveway. I thought I was watching a 1970s cop show. Who does that so brazenly these days? As it happens it was someone who sits a few desks away from me so I went back to the driveway after I had parked my car and picked up his cigarette butt with a tissue, then delivered it to him at his desk and said, 'I think you dropped this.' I embarrassed him in front of co-workers, which in hindsight probably wasn't the best course of action, but I'm pretty sure he's never thrown a cigarette butt out his car window again.

When I see someone drop something in the street I often say to them in an ever-so-polite voice, 'Excuse me, but I think you dropped something,' as though the item they dropped might be precious and I'm doing them a favour by telling them. It doesn't often work and most of the time I get told to go fuck myself, but at least I feel like I have made an attempt to stop the litter problem, short of actually picking up other people's litter (which I do at work, at home and on occasion at my local park, by the way).

If you enjoy your city's parks and beaches then take your rubbish with you when you leave if you can't find a bin nearby.

M

MAKE SOMEONE'S DAY

Not long ago I bought a pair of jeans from a department store. I tried them on, the fit was fine, so I took them to the counter to pay for them. Transaction completed, the salesperson handed me my credit card and my purchase and we both said the requisite thank-yous. Then he said to me, 'And may I just say you are looking particularly suave today.' I was completely taken aback by his comment, mainly because he was about twenty years old and I didn't think twenty-year-olds used words like suave. It wasn't a sales pitch, he was just being nice. The point is, it made my day. I walked away from that store and went back to work feeling great about myself. It didn't cost the person who said it anything but it left me with a good feeling about myself and the department store. Complimenting someone on their appearance or their shoes, or glasses or handbag, makes that person feel good, and I don't mean to sound corny, but maybe they will in turn make someone else feel great, or be so full of bonhomie that they hold the door open for someone when they go through it, or think twice before texting and walking at the same time – or perhaps that's expecting too much?

MEETINGS

They can be one of the most tedious aspects of working life and sometimes it can feel like your whole job is going to meetings rather than getting stuff done. Like it or not, they are a fact of life and the best thing you can do is make them go as smoothly and productively as possible. I once went to a meeting at a major Australian company where there was a sign in the meeting room that said 'Meetings at [this company] start on time and finish on time.' We've all got other things to do, so keeping people waiting is not the most productive way to occupy staff members. If there are ten people in a meeting and it has to start ten minutes late because someone is still in another meeting or stuck in traffic, then nine people have each wasted ten minutes. That's ninety minutes of company time. How much has that cost your business? I say start on time and teach the latecomer a lesson – unless of course that person happens to be the boss or the person who called the meeting in the first place, in which case you are stuck there waiting.

When the meeting starts don't waste more time – end the chitchat and get down to business. Don't talk over the top of people; and don't let the conversation get off track. If you're giving a presentation and there is technology involved then arrive early and make sure it is working properly.

Don't use time in meetings to answer emails, send text messages or tweet something. We're all busy and all have things we need to be doing. If you can attend to your emails while you're in a meeting then chances are you are superfluous to the meeting and would probably be better off not attending. Only having the essential bodies in a meeting will ensure that the meeting time is spent productively.

When setting up a meeting, suggest some dates and times so that the other people involved only have to choose rather than second-guess what will suit you, and you can avoid a whole lot of emails back and forth. Then when it's agreed – or before – inform them you will send a meeting request to make it easier to get it into their diary.

When you send a meeting request, write it as though you are putting it in their diary rather than yours (which you are). For example, if I have a meeting with John Smith and I send him a meeting request that says 'Meeting with John Smith', it's going to mean very little to him, especially if the meeting is some time away. You can later edit the entry in your own calendar and save it just for yourself. Give people a brief reason for the meeting, or send them the agenda if there is one. Send them the correct address, including a Google Maps link if possible, and a contact number for the organiser. If your office building is difficult to find or has complex security then let people know any of the peculiarities they may encounter in advance – the fewer problems there are on the day, the more likely it is that the meeting will start on time.

MOBILE PHONES

When I told people I was writing another guide to modern manners one of the first things people said to me was, 'Are you going to address the issue of mobile phones?'

I like my mobile phone and was an early adopter of the technology. I think of my phone almost like an extension of my body. I rarely leave home without it and on the occasions that I do it is never intentional. One of the reasons I love my mobile phone so much is that a phone today is so much more than a phone and, in fact, making calls is one of the things I use it for least frequently.

There's an episode of *Family Guy* where, in a cutaway clip from the main story, Alexander Graham Bell and Thomas A. Watson are celebrating the success of the first ever telephone call with a drink by the fire.

Watson then asks Bell about a prank phone call he received earlier of a sexually explicit nature (it's *Family Guy*, remember) and Bell pretends he knows nothing about it. 'Probably just some teenagers somewhere, damn them,' he says, brushing it off. 'That's the thing,' Watson says. 'There's only two phones in the world and one of them's in my office and the other's in your office, and those two didn't even exist until about a few hours ago.' 'Yikes, I could use a distraction right now,' says Bell. Although it's *Family Guy* and inherently silly, there is a point to be made here: telephones have been causing people angst since they first came into use.

In the late nineteenth century some people genuinely believed that communicable diseases could be spread over telephone lines, and cautioned against using them.

The invention of the telephone meant that conversations between two people no longer took place in public where, at that time, there were all manner of rules of etiquette that governed how people should behave, as well as how, when, and in what context they could talk to someone. The telephone broke down those rules and people worried it would be the end of civilisation. People saw the phone as an intrusion and didn't want one in their homes. The line between public and private became blurred, and the mobile phone has blurred that line even further because of its portability. There's no point in worrying that mobile phones will have a detrimental impact on society – they are clearly an instrument that has made our lives easier, for the most part. We just need to exercise some common sense and empathy for other people when we use them.

I'm old. I can remember a time when people didn't use their mobile phones at their desk. At the dawn of the new millennium, if you had a mobile you were part of the minority. Only important people like CEOs had their mobile numbers on their business cards. Work calls were done on a landline and your voicemail was an important business tool for picking up calls missed when you were not at your desk. But everyone has a mobile now and landlines have become the minority – I don't have a landline at home and haven't had one for more than ten years. I do have a landline at work, although I can't say I answer it that often. Until quite recently people would call someone on their landline first and if there was no answer they would leave a message or hang up and try again later – they might even send an email instead of leaving a message. You wouldn't call someone's mobile phone until sufficient time had passed to know for certain the person was out of the office and not just in a meeting, in the bathroom or out to lunch. You only called someone on their mobile first if the matter was of extreme urgency. These days those courtesies seem to have been dispensed with and the mobile phone is the first option for many callers.

There's little point in bemoaning this fact as landlines are definitely for the scrapheap in the near future and, as I said, I rarely answer my work landline anyway unless I know who is calling. That's the beauty of mobile phones – unless someone has a private number, you know who is calling you. So I don't mind if people call me on my mobile first so long as they respect a few rules.

If it's work-related don't call outside of business hours unless it's urgent.

If I don't answer leave a message or send me a text – don't keep calling and hanging up until I answer.

If you do send a text then it's a good idea to say who you are – if the person receiving the text doesn't have your number stored in their phone they will have no idea who the message is from.

Here are ten occasions when you should exercise caution in using your mobile phone.

1. In a cinema or theatre. Don't use it for texting or making calls or googling anything. Switch it off and enjoy the movie.
2. During a job interview. I once had someone come and see me who was looking for work and he sent text messages during the meeting. If he couldn't give me his undivided attention for a few minutes – at a meeting he asked for – then why would I trust him with freelance work? There are plenty of other equally qualified people looking for work and, personally, I'm going to choose one with a better attention span.

3. In a library. Turn your phone to silent and only use it for text messaging or data services. Don't make calls.

4. During a first date. Even if you did meet online or via a dating app, be in the moment and give the person your complete attention. Switch your phone to silent and don't take calls while you're on the date.

5. In a museum or art gallery. Switch your phone to silent, only use it for text messaging and data services. If you get a call or need to make one, leave the exhibition.

6. At a place of worship. Switch your phone to silent and only use it for text messages and data services if you are visiting the church to admire its architecture and design – in other words, as a tourist. If you're there as a worshipper then put your phone away.

7. When you are having a conversation with a friend. Nothing says 'you're not that important to me' quite like answering a phone call or sending a text message without excusing yourself before you do it.

8. When you're in a shop and you want to pay for something, or ask a sales assistant for help. Having a conversation on the phone while you pay for something is just plain rude. Call your friend back or wait until the call is over before you go to the counter.

9. While driving a car, unless you have an inbuilt hands-free system.
10. On a plane. Sadly, in the not-too-distant future we will be able to use our phones to make calls and use data services in the air in the same way we can on the ground. In the meantime, pay attention during the safety briefing and switch your phone to flight mode when you are asked to.

Mobile phones have freed us from the shackles of our desk and they have also more or less made the concept of a nine-to-five working day redundant. We all get important phone calls from time to time and if there is something happening in your life on a particular day that means you might have to interrupt a social outing to answer a call or text, then letting people know in advance avoids the possibility of causing offence.

MOBILE PHONES AT THE DINNER TABLE

I was at a lunch not long ago where the waiter had to manoeuvre six mobile phones out of the way so he could place the food on the table. It's become more of a problem as mobile phone screens have got bigger. I must admit that I occasionally put my mobile phone on the dinner table but mostly it's due to a lack of anywhere else to put it. Like I said, phones have got bigger and they are harder to keep in your pocket when you're sitting down. That said, I sometimes have it on the table even when I have a bag at my feet.

In my home mobile phones are banned at the dinner table but for some reason they find their way onto the table when we're in restaurants. If you're dining alone then do what you like – in fact, reading on your phone is a great way to amuse yourself when you are dining solo and you don't need good lighting to be able to read it. But for the times when you're with company, here are some rules about the use of mobile phones at the dinner table.

1. The phone should be face down – unless you're a parent who has left young children at home with a babysitter and they might need to contact you, or you're a doctor on call.

2. If you are expecting an important call then tell your dinner companions at the beginning of the meal and excuse yourself when your phone rings to answer your call away from the table. Likewise, if you're expecting an important text then excuse yourself when you attend to it.

3. Periodically checking your emails while you're at dinner might give your companions the impression you're bored with their company. Checking Instagram or Facebook definitely gives that impression. If you really can't stand not checking Instagram, Facebook or your emails for the duration of the meal then take your phone with you when you go to the bathroom and check it there.

4. For business lunches the rules can be a little more relaxed as you are on work time, but do try to devote the majority of your attention to the business lunch.

For weekend dinners with friends these rules should be strictly adhered to. We all lead busy lives and sometimes coordinating everyone's schedules and dietary requirements to be at the same restaurant at the same time is nothing short of a miracle. Don't waste time looking at emails that can wait until later.

See also PHOTOS OF YOUR FOOD.

MONEY

Talking about money – unless you're talking broadly about the economy – is crass. Of course people are curious about how much money you make or how much you spent on your last holiday, but they don't actually want to listen to you go on about it. Similarly, it's poor form to ask someone about their income or how much something cost.

If you do want to ask someone how much they spent on something then there are two things you can do to avoid sounding like you're just being nosy. The first one is to search online and see if you can find out for yourself. If you want to know how much someone paid for their new house there are ways to do this, and the simplest is to call the real estate agent who sold it to them. Real estate agents can be very obliging, especially if they think you might be a prospective client. If you still can't work it out and you have a genuine need to know – for example, if you bought something similar recently and you're concerned that you might have paid too much – then find a way to ask politely and do it privately rather than at a group gathering. Lead people into the conversation. 'Do you mind if I ask you a personal question?' is a good opener. 'How much did you pay for your father's funeral?' I use that as an example because a friend asked me this when his father passed away shortly after mine. Given that it's not something that most people have much experience in paying for, he wanted to know if the price he was being quoted was reasonable. And of course I was more than happy to share the information with him.

MOVIES

It goes like this: watch movie, discuss later. Don't talk in the movies – ever. Whatever you have to say can always wait unless it's something like 'I think I'm having a heart attack.' Asking your movie companion 'What was she in?' several times throughout a movie is annoying for the person being asked and the people sitting in front of and behind you. Just make a mental note to ask later or look on IMDB. Speaking of looking on IMBD, that's really something that should be done after the movie too. As the screens on smartphones have got bigger so too has the light emanating from their screens become brighter. I know from experience that the home screen on my phone is bright enough to guide me through a darkened forest or to read a restaurant menu by, so it's too bright to use in a movie theatre.

Texting in movies once the main feature has started is for morons. Why would you pay twenty dollars to go to see a movie and then look at your phone instead? Nor do the people around you want to be distracted by the light from your screen while they are trying to watch the film. The problem of people texting in cinemas has become so bad that in the United States some cinema chains have trialled 'phone-friendly sessions', and 'texting seats', whereby the back rows of its cinemas are reserved for patrons who want to text. In some proposed models, those seats could be surrounded with soundproofing to silence any noise, and barriers to dim the glow from mobile phone screens. In the absence of such measures, however, phones should remain in your bag unless you have to leave the cinema to take an important call. Turn your phone to silent if you can't bear to turn it off completely, but if you're not expecting an urgent call, turning it off, or switching it to aeroplane mode, is actually a better option at the movies, because then your calls go straight to voicemail, which notifies your callers that you're unavailable. That way your phone won't buzz through a dozen redials and 'Where are you?' texts.

Feet go on the floor, and gum goes in the bin, not under the seats, along with any other rubbish or food you brought into the cinema with you. Yes, there are people who come in after each movie and clean the cinema, but that's no excuse for leaving more popcorn on the floor than you put in your stomach. The longer it takes for the cinema to be cleaned the longer the next session waits to get in and see their movie. Another way to think of it is this: most cinemas only allocate ten minutes' cleaning time between sessions, so if those staff are focused on cleaning the obvious things like spilled popcorn and leftover rubbish, the less chance there is that they will have time to focus on less obvious things that will make for a more enjoyable viewing experience.

While on the topic of popcorn: if it's possible to eat it quietly then please do so. I'm not a popcorn eater but it does seem to me to be a loud food. I guess keeping one's mouth closed while chewing would be a good start. If you have purchased food with noisy wrappers or packaging, either open these before the movie starts or do it as quickly as possible during the movie. It might seem like unwrapping a lolly very slowly will make the noise less obtrusive but it actually just draws it out and makes the experience more agonising. Like ripping off a Band-Aid, do it quickly. Another good idea is to open noisy food when there is a noisy scene in the movie.

For some reason the no-talking rule seems very difficult to enforce in a home environment. I have a certain friend who talks incessantly in movies when we watch them at his place and it has gotten to the point where I no longer watch a movie with him unless it's something I have no real interest in seeing. The great thing about watching a movie at home is that you can pause it, and doing so when someone is talking is a great, if slightly passive aggressive, way to let them know you'd rather watch now, talk later. But generally speaking the person who owns the television gets to operate the remote control, and if they are also the person talking then weigh up whether it's worth saying something or just catching up on the parts of the movie you missed at a later date. Shushing just makes more noise and can lead to some people sulking and, therefore, not enjoying the movie.

MOVIES ON AN AEROPLANE

See IN-FLIGHT ENTERTAINMENT.

N

NAMES

'Do you mind if I call you Dave?' a call-centre operator asked me recently, when I rang to find out why a technician had failed for a third time to turn up at my house to fix my internet connection. At the time I was just keen to get the problem resolved and I didn't want to get into a conversation about my name actually being David and only my close friends and family calling me Dave. He was just trying to be super-friendly and was no doubt following a call-centre service manual, but in a professional sense nothing leaves a worse impression than getting someone's name wrong.

If someone introduces themselves as Elizabeth, then call them Elizabeth until they ask you to do otherwise. If you have an email relationship with someone and their name is, say, Oliver, and eventually they start signing off as Ollie, then it's fine to start using that version of their name. It doesn't bother me if someone calls me Dave, but I know plenty of people with names that can be easily shortened but they prefer not to. And, yes, sometimes it just sounds like a mouthful, or overly formal, to have to keep calling someone Nicholas or Christopher or Margaret, but that's their name and if that's what they want to be called, then so be it. And shortening names is one thing, but lengthening them is another altogether. If someone's name is Sam, then it's Sam and not Sammy, unless they make it clear that's what they want to be called.

Getting someone's name right is important. If you're introduced to someone and you didn't quite catch their name, then ask them to repeat it. If it's a difficult name to pronounce then say it back to them and ask them if you got it right. Some people are particular about how their name is pronounced and it can become a bugbear for them. If you're one of those people – and I say this as someone with a last name that is not pronounced as it is written – then it's fine to correct them if it bothers you, but in some circumstances it can just make you look like a pedant. Does it really matter if the person at the airport check-in doesn't pronounce your name perfectly? You'll probably never see them again.

A good way to remember someone's name is to use it once or twice in conversation with them, but using it too much can make you sound like you're working in a call centre. In a professional setting, make sure you have someone's name written correctly before you hit send on an email. There are several ways to spell certain popular names – Catherine, Katherine, Kathryn – so don't just assume you have the right one. Check it before you send it.

NEW RELATIONSHIPS

When someone in your social circle starts a new relationship it's important to make the new person feel welcome in your group. In the early days of the relationship if you invite your friend somewhere, and it's an invitation that would normally be for both members of a couple, but you're unsure whether or not they want to be thought of as a couple yet, then the most polite thing to do is just ask one of them, 'Would X like to come too?' That leaves it up to your friend in the new relationship to decide.

After a certain point, however, you need to stop thinking of your friend as single and view them as part of a couple. Of course there is no strict time frame on this but if two people are spending a lot of time together it will become pretty obvious they are a couple now.

If you are one of the people in the new relationship and you find that your friends are leaving your new partner out of invitations then it's probably an oversight and out of habit more than anything else. Don't be afraid to say something to a sympathetic friend – they can then spread the word for you.

O

OBSESSED

Have you noticed that everyone is obsessed with things these days? 'I'm obsessed with those shoes', 'Avocado on toast is my new obsession', 'I'm obsessed with *RuPaul's Drag Race*' (I am), or 'I'm obsessed with sparkling mineral water' (which I heard in a restaurant once). If you're someone who likes to use the word a lot then maybe you should look it up in a dictionary. An obsession is a persistent idea or thought dominating a person's mind and often affecting their behaviour. Do you really think about Gigi Hadid's hair all that persistently?

Overusing the world obsession devalues it. It's like swearing. The more you use certain four-letter words the less potency they have, and then when you really want to express your displeasure at something or someone you are left with no powerful or shocking words in your vocabulary. Save 'obsessed' for when you really are, and in the meantime use other expressive words such as like, love, or adore. Mix it up a little and remember that sometimes words that make good hashtags sound moronic when they are spoken out loud.

OFFICE KITCHENS

My desk is adjacent to an office kitchen and it's a rather disgusting neighbour. I hardly ever go in there as I never take my lunch to work; I prefer to buy it on the day, which has the added benefit of taking me away from the office for a few minutes. So I am basing my view about the use of office kitchens purely on smell. It wouldn't be so bad if it was just one person heating up last night's Indian takeaway for lunch, but just going by my nose what seems to happen is myriad different cuisines get heated in the office microwave throughout the day and, as the office does not have windows, the aromas mesh together and then linger. I mean, seriously, what's wrong with a simple, odourless sandwich? I have no issue with aromatic foods per se, I just have an issue being able to smell it while I'm trying to work. If you do heat up food in the office make an attempt to retrieve it from the microwave as soon as it's done – don't walk away while it's reheating and forget about it – and take it elsewhere to eat, preferably not at your desk. Clean up any mess you make in the kitchen. Don't leave food in the communal fridge to fossilise beyond recognition so the cleaner or a co-worker needs to don a hazmat suit in order to throw it away. Don't leave your dirty plates in the sink to clean up later because you really have to get that report done. If you don't have enough time to clean up after yourself then you don't have enough time for lunch. And don't steal someone else's food no matter how delicious it looks.

OFFICE TEMPERATURE

See SINGLETS OR TANK TOPS.

OPEN-PLAN OFFICES

Management experts will tell you that open-plan offices are all about creating flatter management structures, eliminating office hierarchies and enabling better communication between employees, but anyone who's ever had to work in one knows that's a load of rubbish. Standard open-plan design is essentially about fitting more people into the same amount of floor space than if they were in individual offices. That and the fact it makes the configuration of your office more flexible to suit the changing needs of your business.

The benefits to a company's bottom line mean that the trend is no longer a trend, it's the norm. Facebook's new Frank Gehry–designed workplace in Silicon Valley, for example, is said to have the world's largest open-plan office, with almost three thousand people working together. Despite the omnipresence of open-plan workplace design, some research in the area has revealed that we, the workers, were right all along: it's a crap situation. A story in *The New Yorker* in 2014 concluded that the benefits in building more camaraderie between co-workers is outweighed by the negative impact an open-plan office has on work performance. It damages attention spans, reduces productivity and limits creativity, and has an overall negative impact on job satisfaction. A story in *The Washington Post* in the same year looked at a report by two University of Sydney academics, which found more than half of the workers in the study said that distractions resulting from the lack of sound privacy was the leading cause of frustration in open-plan offices and that it led to poorer work performance. More than thirty per cent of the workers surveyed also cited the lack of visual privacy as a problem.

We know we can't do anything about open-plan office design – apart from working from home, or getting in early or staying back late – so we need to find a way to deal with it.

Sound issues are the main concern for most people so, basically, keep the noise down. If you need to talk to someone at their desk then speak quietly. If you talk on the phone, again, do it as quietly as possible.

If it's a bad line and you need to shout to be heard then hang up and call back from a place designated for making personal calls. Don't shout across the office to someone. Get out of your seat and go to speak to them at their desk, or send them an email. Turn your mobile phone to silent or turn the ringtone down to low – if you're next to it all day it doesn't need to sound like a fire alarm when it rings. You cannot do speakerphone calls at your desk.

Music at your desk without using headphones is an absolute no-no. I once sat next to the music reviewer of a newspaper I used to work for and if he can wear headphones, everyone can. Just don't sing along with the music. If you see someone at their desk with headphones on typing away at their computer or reading, then avoid breaking their concentration. Send them an email and ask to see them when they are free. If the matter is urgent then gently tapping them on the shoulder to get their attention is fine. Although the noise in an open-plan office can be a distraction, you shouldn't have your music so loud that you're completely unaware of what's going around you or can't hear your phone ring.

Everyone likes to take a break from work every now and then and check in with social media. It's a good idea to leave a set of headphones permanently plugged into your computer so you can avoid annoying the office when a video autoplays. If you see something hilarious you don't need to shout to the entire office that they need to come and check this out. If you do check your Facebook or Twitter at work then shut it down when you leave your desk. In fact, logging out of your computer is a good thing to do if you are going to lunch or to a meeting and you have sensitive documents open that you're working on.

Use dedicated meeting areas if your office has them rather than conducting meetings at your desk. If a meeting organically forms at your desk and it looks like the conversation is going to go for more than a minute or two, suggest to the group that you all go somewhere else.

Sometimes a short team chat about what everyone watched on television the night before is a welcome break from your work, but if you sense that others nearby are trying to get something done to meet a deadline then take it elsewhere or cut it short.

If you need to make a personal phone call on work time, you have a mobile phone so get mobile with it and go outside or to a quiet place. This also helps to safeguard your privacy. If people do make private phone calls at work – or even work-related calls – try to avoid listening in, and if you do overhear a conversation don't contribute to it after the call has ended as you will just look like a busybody. If you're going to tell a little white lie on the telephone – such as you didn't call so-and-so back earlier because you were out of the office all day yesterday when in fact you weren't – inform those within earshot first so they don't burst into laughter when you do it and blow your cover.

The reality of office life is that people will eat at their desks even if separate eating areas are provided, because people have work to do and they want to keep going with it rather than taking a lunch break. This is precisely why some employers provide food-preparation facilities in their offices, because ultimately it's good for productivity. If you do eat at your desk, try to avoid eating overly aromatic food, and remove your plate and clean up as soon as you're done. If you have a rubbish bin at or near your desk, then this is not the place to dispose of smelly food. Take it to the kitchen and put it in the bins there. If you hot-desk then wipe down the desktop surface at the end of the day.

OVERHEAD LOCKERS ON AEROPLANES

Are there to share. One of the reasons I like to board a flight as early as possible – in fact it's the only reason – is that if you don't then you're often faced with the likelihood of the overhead locker near you being full. There is a limit set on how much cabin baggage passengers can take on board and I think it's safe to believe that if everyone limited themselves to that amount as a maximum then there would be room enough for everyone's things. Cabin baggage has become an issue, particularly on short-haul domestic flights, as many airlines now charge for checked baggage, especially on their budget fares. So to get around that passengers try to cram more than their allocated share of cabin baggage into the overhead lockers. For the sake of other passengers you should only take the allocated amount, which is clearly detailed at the time of booking. If you know you will have more than that amount then pay for a checked bag then and there – it's often much cheaper to do it in advance rather than waiting until check-in.

Personally I like to take the least amount of cabin baggage as possible, for two reasons. First, the less I have the easier it will be to stow in the overhead locker and, second, the less I have the easier it is to carry. I hate the idea of having to schlep bags through airports from one gate to the next and the few times I've done it – when trying to travel with hand luggage only using a small wheelie case – I've always had the misfortune of having to go up and down stairs. And if you have a case without wheels, chances are you'll be landing at gate 1 and getting your connecting flight from gate 2000 (or at least it seems that way).

I travel a lot for work and while I don't claim to be an expert on how to travel well, there are a few tips I've picked up on the way. One piece of advice I would offer is that trying to travel with just hand luggage isn't worth it. Even if I'm only going away for one night I check my bag in because it makes my time in the airport terminal that much easier. If you've ever travelled on your own and had hand luggage on wheels as well as another bag, and tried to use a public toilet, then you'll know what I mean. Also, who would even want to wheel a bag into a public toilet? If the majority of your luggage is checked, you don't need to worry about this problem.

But that's just one reason why I don't travel with only hand luggage. I do approximately one long haul flight per month as well as a few shorter trips in between. In all my travel I have had my bags go missing twice – on one occasion my bag turned up at my office a couple of hours later and the other it was about twenty-four hours later. Yes, it was an inconvenience, but it wasn't the end of the world. As much fun as travelling is there's a hell of a lot of wasted time queuing, looking for somewhere to sit, walking from gate to gate or just standing around, and as far as I'm concerned the less stuff I have to carry or worry about the more enjoyable the experience will be. So, yes, I'm prepared to risk my bags being delayed for the sake of personal comfort.

And, really, how busy are you that you can't wait a few minutes for your bag at the other end? All you have to do is factor the waiting time into your schedule. Some people will read this and disagree, but it works for me. I sometimes look at people in airports and marvel at the amount of stuff they are struggling to carry with them onto a plane and think, why would you bother? The most amazing thing about these people laden with luggage is they usually have checked in luggage as well. I'm a heavy packer but there is such a thing as taking too much with you.

The same rules apply to travelling on buses and trains. For trains the baggage limits seem to be far less strictly enforced, but there is still limited space for large suitcases. If one passenger hogs all the space with an excessive amount of luggage, then everyone else is inconvenienced. You should also be mindful that you will have to lift your bag on and off the carriage yourself, so if you can't carry it then don't take it.

OVERSHARING

Some things – such as close-up photos of horrific dental work – do not need to be shared on social media. As I write this section I am trying to stop myself from throwing up, as I have just seen a photo on Facebook of the inside of someone's mouth with a pussy abscess. I mean, I've been there and had painful dental work before, so I sympathise a little, but no one – and I mean no one – apart from your dentist should have to look at that. And who took this photo? Did you ask the nurse to do it?

From what I've been able to observe from following what turns out to be a lot of rather needy people on social media, it seems that oversharing, particularly of traumatic, depressing or difficult things, is motivated by a need for sympathy and attention. I know someone on Facebook who has the body of a god and he posts a lot of photos of himself with his shirt off. And why wouldn't he? He looks amazing. But the captions often go something like this: 'Skipped the gym today and had ice-cream instead. Yikes!'. The response he is trying to illicit is along the lines of 'You look awesome!' or 'OMG, you're so hot' or, better yet, just a fire emoji. And he gets those comments, in spades.

If you're an oversharer out of a need for sympathy or attention then you might start to lose followers – or, worse, people might start talking about you and your posts for all the wrong reasons. Despite the fact that social media has allowed us to share every intimate moment of our lives online with people we might not know, a little bit of mystery can go a long way. Some things, like the graphic details of your root canal work, are best kept to yourself.

P

PALE SUITS

Barack Obama learned the hard way what happens when you try something different with your wardrobe when he shocked the American public by wearing a tan suit to a press conference in 2014. The press conference was actually about his government's strategy for tackling ISIS, but all anyone could talk about was his tan suit. Newspapers such as *The Washington Post* weighed in on the suit, as did *Time* and *Esquire*. The White House even made a joke about it on its official Twitter account in the lead up to the subsequent State of the Union address and posted a picture of the suit on a hanger, suggesting that Obama would wear it to deliver his speech, with the hashtag #YesWeTan.

The point is, Obama's choice of suit at his press conference was considered controversial and it overshadowed what he was saying. Very few people can pull off a tan suit, so they are best avoided. For some reason men seem to want to wear pale suits for special occasions such as their wedding, and the problem with that is on special occasions people take photographs, so the fashion crime will be remembered for years to come. Just remember that navy blue is a colour that suits everyone and is suitable for every occasion. Black is best for evening suits such as a tuxedo. Dark grey or very dark brown can also look good on anyone. Pulling off a light- or bright-coloured suit takes chutzpah, which means you need it to wear it with killer shoes, shirt and tie, and it needs to be tailored to perfection. Tailoring can take the same suit from daggy to Fashion with a capital F.

PARTIES AT HOME

I love organising and planning a party, but there is always that moment just before your guests arrive when everything is under control – the house is tidy, the flowers look amazing, the table is set and everything is where it should be – that I sometimes feel like calling it all off and just enjoying the state of pre-party bliss my house is in. When you're hosting a party at home, whether it's big or small, the ambience and the people you invite are far more important than your cooking. If you go to some effort to make your home look a little bit special – buy some flowers, set the table, employ a waiter for a special occasion – then people will forgive all manner of shortcomings when it comes to the food. People have come to your home to have a good time – if they want an haute culinary experience then they will go to a restaurant.

You should always serve plenty of good-quality drink – because just as people will overlook a slightly overcooked roast if the table setting is perfection, so they will if you serve a special bottle of wine or two.

Greet your guests as they arrive. If you have a big house and it's going to be a big party then stand near the front door as your guests arrive to greet them – don't make them hunt you down. It also helps ease any anxiety that guests who might not know anyone else at your party feel about arriving alone and seeking out the host.

Don't let people clean up as the guests are leaving and don't start doing it yourself – it's a sure-fire way to kill the mood. That said, if you want people to leave and they won't, then turning up the lights and starting the clean-up is a polite way of saying, 'It's time to go.'

Try not to have too many rules. No smoking in the house is perfectly acceptable – and most people will go outside anyway – but insisting on no red wine, no stilettos or no shoes at all makes you look like a bit of a killjoy. If your home is so precious that you need to stipulate rules for anyone who enters then maybe consider hiring a venue for your next party.

People always think about the music, but think about the lighting as well. It shouldn't be too bright, or so dark that people trip over the furniture. You want the light to be flattering. Avoid using overhead lighting unless it can be dimmed. Lamps placed around the room are best, but if you don't have enough lamps you can always use candlelight. If you've invited people over for drinks or dinner then they should be able to talk comfortably over the music, and you might need to lower the volume as more people arrive.

Think about the seating, especially if it's a big group. You don't need to set out place cards, just tell people where you would like them to sit. In 2016 *The New York Times* profiled Lady Elizabeth Anson, who has been Queen Elizabeth the Second's party planner for more than fifty years. In the interview she shared some of her top tips for hosting the perfect party. As well as the importance of lighting, which she said can make or break a party, her number one piece of advice is to seat all the bores together. 'They don't realise they're the bores and they're happy. It's my biggest tip,' she said.

PETROL STATIONS

At a petrol station recently the man waiting behind me decided to drive around to the exit of the petrol station and then back up in front of me to use the spare bowser (there was a car at this bowser when I pulled in to the petrol station that had since departed). His action locked me in until he was finished. I was so infuriated that I asked him why he did that, and told him I had every intention of moving forward as soon as I had filled my car and before I went in to pay. 'I'm in a hurry,' was his lame response. There is a queueing system at a petrol station, just as there is everywhere else in life. In Sydney, where I live, petrol stations seem to be becoming rarer by the day, especially around the inner city. They occupy large parcels of land and perhaps that land is more valuable as an apartment block than a petrol station, which means there is even greater demand on the existing petrol stations and a queue is a given. If you're in a hurry and running low on petrol, then the only advice I can offer is to leave the house a few minutes earlier rather than attempt to push your way into what is already a frustrating queue.

PHOTOS AT A FUNERAL

Can you take photographs at a funeral? It all depends on whose funeral it is. I've been to a couple of funerals recently where people were taking photographs – not everyone, like at concerts these days, just the occasional one. The first time I saw it happen I thought it was a little odd. I was at the funeral of a friend's father and the person in front of me at the church took a few photographs with a camera rather than their phone. Afterwards I asked the person who took the photos if she always does that at funerals (curious rather than judgemental) and she told me that the wife of the deceased actually asked her to do so. Her husband was in his eighties when he died and she thought the funeral should be a celebration of his life, and that it would be nice to have some photos of all the people who had gathered for the event, many of whom had not seen each other in years.

Photos at funerals should always be at the request of the family of the deceased. There are times, though, when the family won't want to be bothered with details like that, as organising a funeral is hard work at the best of times. If you think the family would like it but don't want to bother them with the request then there is a way to go about it.

A couple of years ago a friend of mine died – she was my age, so it was a very sad event – and there was a memorial service for her at dawn on a beach. We all gathered and one of my friends, who is an accomplished amateur photographer, brought his camera with him. It was a beautiful spring morning, and people who had not seen each other in years gathered together and he took some great photos – without intruding on others' privacy – and afterwards he told the partner of the deceased that he had done so. He said something along the lines of, 'I took some photos today because I thought you might want them but probably didn't want to think about it. If you'd rather I hadn't I will delete them all, but they are there for you if you want them.' She did want them and was pleased he had the foresight to do it.

I've even been to a funeral – again for someone's father who had led a full life – and one of his children actually took a photo of the entire congregation in the church from the position of the altar. It was early in the service, he told everyone what he was doing and in the resulting photo you can see smiles on everyone's faces. I wouldn't mind if someone did that at my funeral. It's all just a matter of the appropriateness of the situation.

PHOTOS OF YOUR FOOD

When you take photos of food to post online make sure you're wearing clothes, as shiny objects like tea pots and cutlery have a tendency to reflect things. I remember once looking at someone's post of their lovely breakfast setting, which included a shiny silver teapot. Even though it was on Instagram and you couldn't zoom in on the photo at that time, it was clear to everyone who saw it that the photographer was stark naked. Someone quickly alerted him and he promptly deleted the post, but screenshots had already been taken and they will live on in perpetuity. This is just one hazard of posting photos of your food on social media. The other one is that people will find you annoying and possibly limit the time they spend with you eating in restaurants.

If you are going to take a photo of your dinner then do it quickly. You're not Mario Testino and you're not taking photos for *Gourmet Traveller* magazine.

Don't spend eons rearranging the table and adjusting the lighting – just take the damn picture so the rest of your dinner companions can get on with eating. The only thing more annoying than the person who wants to photograph their meal is the person who wants to photograph your meal. A dining companion saying, 'Oh, don't eat anything until I take a picture!' is enough to send me around the bend.

Perhaps stop and think before you take that picture of your meal. Sure it's a great-looking cup of coffee and plate of avocado toast, but is it really so amazing that it needs to be posted to Instagram? Is it the best piece of avocado on toast *ever*? Perhaps just enjoy the moment and eat your breakfast with your partner or friend. And if you are at a dinner with a bunch of people and you want to post a picture of your meal, maybe it can wait until after the meal. Nothing looks more comical than a table of people all looking at their phones while their food in front of them goes cold.

But if you are going to post photos of your food then be creative about it; don't just make it another picture of a perfect latte. Check out the Instagram account instagram. com/symmetrybreakfast if you want to see what a clever and creative food-based Instagram looks like.

POINTING

'Don't point!' is something that was drummed into my mind whenever I would point at something as a child. The problem was that no one offered an alternative, and pointing seemed to me the most efficient way of directing someone's attention towards a particular object. Many people consider pointing with an index finger to be a rude and potentially aggressive act. Personally, I think there are situations where it is fine to point with your index finger. For example, if you are giving a presentation at work and you want to draw the audience's attention to something on the screen, then use your index finger – no one will think it is an aggressive act in this situation. Or if, say, you're in a lighting store and you are trying to explain to the sales assistant which particular light fitting you would like a quote on and there are hundreds hanging from the ceiling, then I think pointing is just going to speed things up and be for the benefit of all concerned. I use this example as, on one particular occasion, the sales assistant I was dealing with clearly had an aversion to pointing, but was trying to draw my attention to various light fittings in the store and I had no idea which ones she was talking about. Pointing in this instance would have been helpful rather than rude.

But, if you're back in that meeting and you want to direct attention to a particular person in the room, and you can't recall their name, then pointing at them with your index finger makes you look a little boorish. First you didn't remember the person's name and now you're pointing at them. In this situation the best way to point is to do it with an open palm and by keeping all the fingers together, in other words, you point with your whole hand.

Some people think pointing is best done with one's little finger. I don't know why, but for some reason I find this method a little creepy. If you're not comfortable pointing with your index finger then use your whole hand in the method described above.

POPCORN

See MOVIES.

PREGNANCY

Never ask a woman if she is pregnant. If a woman you know has suddenly gained weight around her midriff and you suspect she might be expecting, and you really want to know, then, frankly, the issue here is simply one of learning when to mind your own business. She will tell people when she's ready. There are lots of reasons why a woman may want to keep her pregnancy secret for a period of time, but if your curiosity has the better of you then consider asking a mutual friend first before you dive in with, 'So when is the baby due?' If she's not pregnant then you've basically just told her she's gained weight.

You should also never ask someone why she isn't pregnant, or why she hasn't had children. There are many reasons why someone might not have had children and it is possibly a sensitive or upsetting topic for that person. Some people have no issue discussing their problems with conceiving and their experiences of IVF, et cetera, but ultimately it's no one else's business and choosing to discuss the issue is theirs alone.

Don't ask someone who is pregnant or who has just had a child if their baby was conceived through IVF or naturally. If the person wants you to know or thinks it's relevant in some way, then they will tell you.

Don't touch a woman's pregnant belly without asking first (and only if you actually know the person).

Do offer your seat to a pregnant woman on crowded public transport.

And if you're in a long queue for, say, a public toilet and there is a pregnant woman also in the queue, let them go ahead of you.

PUNCTUALITY

See LATENESS.

Q

QUEER

Is it okay to call someone queer? The short answer is no, unless that person has either specifically asked you to refer to them as queer or refers to themselves as queer often enough for it to be clear that they accept the term. It's a politically charged term, and if people want to be referred to that way they will almost certainly be up front about it. 'Queer' used to be a pejorative word used in an umbrella fashion to describe all forms of sexual minorities. In the late 1980s some academics and activists started to reclaim the word in a similar fashion to the way other minorities have made efforts to own words that were once used derisively towards them. However, that doesn't mean that all LGBTI people are okay with being called queer. Some LGBTI people disapprove of the word because they still see it as a form of hate speech, mainly because some people continue to use it that way. Other LGBTI people don't like the word because they associate it with radicalism. Either way, refrain from using it unless you're queer and are okay with it. Find another word. In fact, think about why you need to refer to someone's sexual orientation or gender in the first place.

QUEUE JUMPING

Don't you hate those people who say things like 'I don't like queueing for breakfast' when they get to a cafe and find there is a wait for a table? I've yet to meet anyone who enjoys a good queue. No one likes queues, but they are a fact of life when you live in a big city. Unless you're frail or incapacitated in some way there is no way to bypass the queue without incurring the wrath of everyone else waiting. Running late for an appointment is not a valid queue-jumping excuse. You just have to wait it out.

If you have a legitimate excuse for wanting to go to the front of the line (for example, you have two small children and you are travelling on your own), then ask either the people at the front of the queue or the official managing the queue if it's okay to do so. If the answer is 'yes' then be gracious about it. For the most part people are more than happy to allow someone to go ahead of them if it's clear that person has a genuine need, so a small thank-you wouldn't go astray.

Queueing is unpleasant for everyone and making it more so achieves nothing. Not long ago I arrived in Los Angeles after a long flight from Sydney and was told my connecting flight had been cancelled and I needed to queue to get a new boarding pass for an alternative flight. Everyone on that connecting flight was affected and we all took our places in what was already a long and slow-moving queue. A man came up behind me and said, 'I have a connecting flight, can I go ahead of you?' After I explained (politely) that we all had connecting flights, which is what the queue was for, and that I was approximately person fifty in the queue and going in front of me wasn't really going to achieve much, he huffed and puffed and tapped his feet – none of which made the queue move any faster.

R

RACISM

See X-CULTURAL SENSITIVITIES.

REGIFTING

When it comes to gift-giving, we're told from an early age that it's better to give than to receive. We're also told that it's the thought that counts and we shouldn't look a gift-horse in the mouth. Like all well-worn clichés, there's an element of truth to these and they can apply even to the vexing issue of regifting presents you have received to others – a dilemma that many of us will face throughout the year.

Can you regift something that you don't like/don't need/don't fit or just don't want? Most etiquette books would tell you this is a no-no. I, on the other hand, think it's perfectly acceptable so long as you obey some rules so that no one gets hurt. So let's look at this vexing issue cliché by cliché.

It's better to give than receive: This is absolutely true. But occasionally you can find yourself running late for a party or invited at the last minute, or having just totally forgotten about it, and you haven't had time to get a little host gift for the person throwing the party. Taking a bottle of wine or a sixpack of beer is not a gift – that's just what civilised people do when invited to someone's house. It's a lot of trouble to throw a party, so you need a small token in appreciation of the effort your host has undertaken. This is how I rationalise it: you need to take a gift, you haven't purchased one and you don't have time to go out and get one. You look around the house to see if there's anything with which you can part that would make a nice gift – it's the thought that counts – and so what if that gift is something someone else gave you? You own what you're regifting – it's yours to do whatever you want with.

I have a friend who actually has a cupboard in his house that strangely seems to be filled with books and scented candles. I asked him what it was all about and he was very frank about it. 'It's our regifting cupboard,' he said. 'You know, just because I don't like something doesn't mean someone else won't like it. And I don't like to throw things out.'

It's the thought that counts: True enough, but sometimes people just don't put a lot of thought into their gifts and suddenly you're stuck with more scented candles than you know what to do with and enough beach towels to last a lifetime. So what's wrong with giving one of those things to someone you think might actually like it?

Don't look a gift-horse in the mouth: Remember to always be gracious in accepting a gift no matter how unwanted it may be. Part of being gracious is not hurting someone's feelings. Don't inspect it or ask how much it cost, just accept the gift for what it is.

When regifting, you need to make sure there is absolutely no chance that the person who gave it to you will ever find out. Always regift to someone completely unrelated. If there is any chance that the original giver will find out then you'll need to go shopping and find something else. Save that thing you don't want for regifting on another occasion. That regifting cupboard is starting to sound like a good idea!

It's also important to remember who gave you what. If you're the sort of person who receives a lot of gifts, or if you've recently been married and showered in all manner of household items, then make a note of who gave you what. The only thing worse than the original gifter finding out that you regifted their gift to someone else is giving it back to them.

Back to my friend with the regifting cupboard. He gives me a word of caution about being such an organised regifter. 'We never regift things that the kids were given,' he says. 'They're hopeless at it and blurt out that they were given it by so-and-so and they don't like it. The other kids don't seem to care but their parents start to question everything you've ever given them.'

And that's the key to this issue. Go ahead and do it, just don't let on. You're not being deceitful, you're just avoiding hurting someone's feelings and, yes, making someone else happy. You're also preventing unnecessary waste, and not everything you don't want or need is suitable for donating to charity.

REVOLVING DOORS

These are designed to keep heat in (or out of) a building and also for the speedy egress and ingress of people. I work in a building that has a rather large revolving door leading in and out of the main lobby. The door area is divided into three sections that are big enough to fit several people. Personally I prefer not to enter a section behind other people as I don't like being so close to people unless I know them. But if you are the sort of person who has no problem being in a confined space with strangers then it's a good idea to get out of the way of the building entrance quickly when you leave the door, unless you want people to bump into you. Doors that revolve are like escalators in that there is a constant stream of people exiting them, so don't stand near one just as you wouldn't stand at the end of an escalator.

You should also have your wits about you. That means not staring down at your phone as you try to navigate a revolving door. You might be okay with people bumping into you from behind because you're walking slower than the revolving door is ejecting people, but others are not always pleased with having to trip over someone trying to do two things at once. Put your phone away for a few seconds – what you're looking at can wait, and if it can't then try standing aside and attending to it before you enter the revolving door.

ROAD RAGE

I'm not the best person to comment on road rage, having been known to get frustrated with other drivers and their crappy road skills. However, on the way to Tokyo airport I was recently given a lesson in how best to handle a near-death experience. My taxi driver and another car had a near collision at high speed. The other driver decided at the last minute to abort his exit off the freeway and made a swift turn to the right, nearly sideswiping the car I was in. It all happened quickly and was actually quite scary – I was sure we were going to hit the car, but we didn't. Instead of screaming and flipping fingers at each other the two drivers composed themselves and bowed at each other from behind the wheel and moved on. I would have been more inclined to scream obscenities but they took the higher ground. They didn't even sound their horns.

Now that is probably something that is not going to happen on most city roads, certainly not the city I live in, but you can learn something from that way of handling a near accident.

On another occasion when I was driving, I changed lanes and didn't quite see another car – which, in my defence, was in my blind spot – and narrowly avoided an accident. The other driver decided to get out of his car at the next set of lights and approached my window. I panicked as it was a quiet street and I thought I was in imminent physical danger, so I did the only thing I could think of that might save me: I admitted blame. I said something like, 'I'm so sorry, I didn't see you. It was totally my fault. It's a new car and I can't see a thing out of the back window.' That last bit was a lie but the guy actually took pity on me and said, 'Yeah these [automotive company] cars have shit visibility. At least no one was hurt and no damage was done to your new car.' The point is, driving is fraught with all sorts of dangers and mishaps, and if no one was hurt and no damage was done then that's a good thing and not something that requires a raised finger or a torrent of abuse.

That said, don't be a dick on the road. Don't sit in someone's blind spot, unless you like not being seen.

Let someone in to the queue of traffic – it really won't make much difference to your arrival time. Australian drivers are terrible at this and have perfected the art of staring straight ahead and pretending they can't see you sitting there with your blinker on trying to get into their lane. Italians, on the other hand, are crazy drivers and they do it all at high speed, but they will let you in to a queue of traffic. Just remember what it's like when you're the person trying to change lanes and can't get in – have some empathy and let the person in. Having said that, if someone doesn't indicate that they want to change lanes then bugger them.

Another good tip is to have a crappy car. Years ago I had a rust-bucket Peugeot that was barely roadworthy and looked like a heap of junk, but the engine was good and it kept on going. I realised very quickly that a bad car – one that you wouldn't notice a new scratch on – gives you the freedom to drive less cautiously. People get out of your way when they see you trying to change lanes because they know you have nothing to lose. To this day when I see someone driving in a clapped-out old vehicle I give them plenty of room.

ROAD RULES

If everyone obeyed the rules of the road then there would really be no need for outbursts of road rage. So, to that end . . .

Use your indicator, especially when you are making a right-hand turn, and give plenty of notice – don't just wait until you're already turning to use it. It's called an indicator because it *indicates* to other drivers what your intentions are.

If you find yourself stuck behind some dick who is turning right and hasn't bothered to indicate, the first person behind them is the first one to go around the offending driver, not the second or third or fourth person. A queue is a queue and jumping it is never excusable. If there is one piece of bad behaviour on our roads that really pisses me off it's that one. On a recent trip to Italy I was driving on two-lane highways through the countryside and it took me a while to get used to the fact that when you get stuck behind a slow-moving truck the queue of drivers that quickly forms behind you is actually waiting for you to overtake first – the truck drivers even move as far to the right as possible to let you pass when there is a clear stretch of road. It's the only fair way to do it. Italians as a general rule drive like they are all in Ferraris and Lamborghinis but they do it with civility.

Don't park someone in so tightly that the only way they can get out is to bump in to other cars.

Park within the lines of a parking bay.

Don't double-park and hold up everyone behind you.

Don't text and drive. It's stupid and inconsiderate. Personally I don't care if you get a fine from a police officer for texting and driving, and I don't care if you have an accident while doing it, unless it's me you crash into. The problem I have with people who text and drive is they are hopeless drivers while doing it. Texting takes your eyes off the road so you don't see the lights change to green, which delays everyone behind you. And driving slower when you text doesn't make it safer, it just makes you a slower and more annoying driver. Texting when you're behind the wheel of a car is really just the stupidest thing you can do. And to all those people out there who say, 'But I'm a good multi-tasker and I can do two things at once and I've never had an accident while texting and driving,' take it from me, you're doing at least one of those things badly and it's most likely the driving part. Oh, and everyone behind you hates you.

Road rules are mostly matters of the law but there are some instances where acting like a decent human being (such as letting someone into a queue of traffic) can make the experience of being in busy traffic much more bearable for everyone. But it's only fair that if you break the law when driving, such as doing an illegal U-turn, then you have to give way to other people. You're the one who wants to break the law, don't involve other people in your crime.

See also ZEBRA CROSSINGS.

RSVP

Historically, etiquette books would insist that you respond to an invitation in the same manner in which you received it. That means if it was a hard copy written invitation then you need to respond in hard copy. Today, apart from wedding invitations, that's not necessary and highly impractical. An invitation, even a formal one, should make it clear how the organiser would like to receive a response. It might ask you to reply to a specific email address or telephone number. You should respond as quickly as possible. If it's for a major event, such as a wedding or a milestone birthday party, and you have something that might conflict with it but has not yet been confirmed – for example, a business trip – then it's helpful to let the event organiser know that you have received the invitation, explain your situation and tell them you will confirm as soon as possible.

For more casual events such as a dinner at home a text message is acceptable. If you're the sort of person who still invites people to something over the telephone then it's a good idea not to start the conversation with 'What are you doing next Saturday night?' It can put people in an awkward position if they do not have plans but still wish to be selective about what kind of offers they accept. It's far better to just come straight out with it.

If you're accepting an invitation it is a little rude to ask who else is going to be there as it gives the impression that your attendance will be conditional on the guest list. That said, people do like to know who they are going to be breaking bread with, so as the party planner, why not put people at ease and tell them who else is coming or has been invited? It has the dual effect of preventing an invitee from unwittingly letting someone know about a party that they haven't been invited to and creating unnecessary tension.

S

SAVE THE DATE

Sometimes I feel like I get more save the dates than I do actual invitations. I always find them kind of impertinent. They almost yell at you when they arrive in your mailbox – virtual or physical. 'SAVE THE DATE', they demand. What about 'SAVE THE DATE PLEASE'? Or 'Please save the date'? That's all it takes, a six letter word, to transform your directive to block out time in my busy calendar from domineering to delightful. And what do you do when you've been asked to (please) save the date for an event that is off in the never-never and an actual invitation never shows up, and you don't notice until the day before the event? Or worse, when you see photos from the event on social media and suddenly recall getting a save the date for that party?

Chalk it down to an oversight and enjoy an evening in front of the TV. If you're a party planner you should make sure that the list of people you send a save the date to is the same as the list of people who you send the actual invitation to.

A save the date notice should not take the place of an invitation – if you intend for it to be the actual invitation then call it that rather than a save the date. Asking someone to kindly save the date implies that an invitation is on its way. Similarly, it's just a save the date, so you don't need to RSVP until the formal invitation arrives. If you get more than one save the date or invitation to an event on the same day you can choose which one you want to go to, and you shouldn't try to do everything. It's actually much more helpful for a party organiser to get a 'no' rather than a 'I have another party on that night but I will try to get to yours later.'

SEAT RECLINING

This has become a big issue recently and it's odd because airline seats have reclined ever since commercial planes first took to the skies. But in the last decade or so airlines changed how they think about the people flying on their planes. No longer do they refer to people as 'passengers' – these days you're a 'customer'. The change is more than a semantic one. Passenger implies a duty of care and customer suggests that the relationship is purely transactional. In the mind of the customer it says that 'I paid for my seat and I'm entitled to recline it.' That's all well and good, but the person sitting behind you is also convinced they paid for their seat and personal space, and is entitled to not be infringed upon. As I've mentioned elsewhere in this book, airlines are profit-driven businesses, and one of the best ways to increase profit is to get more people on the aircraft, which means leg room in economy class is even tighter than it used to be.

Here's the reality: If you weren't meant to recline in an airline seat then they wouldn't come with a recline function. However, that doesn't mean you shouldn't exercise some common courtesy when you decide you want to lie back and relax. Just as you would look behind you when reversing in a car, be aware of what is going on in the seat to your rear. It's a nice gesture to inform the person behind you that you would like to recline your seat. You don't need to ask permission, you just need to give the other person a heads up. If your fellow passenger is working on their laptop then recline slowly. If it's mealtime then wait until the meal service is finished before you recline, even if you're not eating. It's like a chain reaction, so recline your own seat the way you would want the passenger in front of you to do it. If you're the person in the reclined seat then don't get hot under the collar when the person behind you has to grab the top of your seat to get in or out, as there really is no alternative.

I find it hard to understand the recent furores around seat-reclining on planes because, as I said before, economy class seats are built with a recline function so it's designed to be used. If you really can't abide the practice then here are two pieces of advice. Number one: book the row behind the exit row, as exit row seats in economy class can't be reclined. Number two: if you want privacy and personal space on an aircraft then, as a general rule, you won't find it in economy class. We're all in the same boat, so you'll need to suck it up or find another way to travel.

SELFIES AND SELFIE STICKS

On a recent holiday in Europe I felt like I was the only one without a selfie stick. My holiday didn't suffer because of it, and there are still a few selfies of me and my partner from the trip somewhere in my phone. When people look back on this decade in years to come I think they will say that the dumbest invention of our time is the selfie stick (followed by a seven hundred dollar hair dryer, but that's another matter entirely). I guess if you were a solo traveller and you wanted to take a few photos of yourself at various places around the world then a selfie stick might be a useful thing. But do you know what's easier than carrying around a selfie stick with you? Asking someone to take your photo. Even if you don't speak the language, it's a pretty easy thing to communicate with gestures.

Judging by the number of people I have encountered using a selfie stick I am clearly in the minority in my dislike of them. If you are going to use one, be mindful and considerate of the people around you. Yes, it's astonishing to see Botticelli's *The Birth of Venus* in the flesh at the Uffizi Gallery in Florence, and of course you want to tell your friends you've seen it, and what better way to prove that than with a photo of you in front of the painting? It means you were really there. Other people, however, are also trying to look at the painting in what is an almost perpetually busy room in a busy museum. Your constant taking and re-taking, and waiting for a break where no one else is in the frame, is having an impact on everyone else's enjoyment. If you must do it, then do it quickly and with a minimum of fuss (and, please, if the gallery you're in has rules about flash photography then please observe them – they are imposed for a reason, and following them will set a good example for others).

Selfie sticks have been banned from several sporting events, such as the Australian Open tennis tournament, because they are distracting to the players and intrusive for other spectators. In places and events where they are not banned, a little common sense would go a long way. If I'm sitting next to you at the cricket then I'd be more than happy to take a photo of you and your girlfriend for you if it meant I didn't have to have my view blocked by your selfie stick jutting out in front of me. And, really, one photo is enough – you've got the shot, now get back to watching the game. It does sometimes seem that the documenting of being somewhere is more important than being there.

Look behind you as you back up when you're setting up a photo with a selfie stick. You don't want to fall off that cliff, at least not until you have the shot.

Don't make a phone call with the selfie stick still attached to your phone. It just looks silly.

SENDING LARGE FILES VIA EMAIL

Once upon a time you couldn't attach any files larger than one megabyte to an email. Today it seems that there's almost no limit on sending size, but that still doesn't mean it's okay to attach a 25 MB file to an email and expect a swift and receptive response. Besides, many companies have server limits that prohibit people from receiving emails over a certain size, so just because you can send it doesn't mean the person receiving it can open it. People who work from home may not have a very fast internet connection, or downloading large files might eat into their data allowance, so only send files that are essential. If someone is travelling and using global roaming the last thing they want to do is download a huge file. And if they're using hotel wi-fi then chances are it is so slow it could take hours to download the file. The best way to manage sending large files is via a cloud-based storage service like Dropbox or WeTransfer (both of which are free for a basic account). That way all you need to do is send a link to the file and the person receiving it can download it at their convenience. It's important to remember there are potential security issues when using third-party services such as these, so either protect your files with a password if the service offers that facility, or find a way to send it to the person directly (for example, create a smaller file).

It's also helpful to the person on the receiving end to know what you are sending them so they can make an informed decision on whether to download it now or wait until they are connected to their company's wi-fi. If it's not immediately important or just being sent FYI then say so in your email.

SEXTING

For those reading this who don't know what the term 'sexting' means, you probably don't need to read any more of this particular entry. Sexting is the practice of sending naked pictures or explicit texts to someone. You go back and forth and whip each other into a frenzy. What can I say? To each their own, and if you're not hurting anyone in the process then knock yourself out. However – I once sat across the aisle from a man on a flight from Melbourne to Sydney and I watched as he went through his camera roll to delete unwanted photos and free up storage space on his phone. I've done this myself when I had nothing better to do, so I watched and thought, 'I'm glad I'm not the only one who does that.' But then I noticed his photos were a little different to mine. Let's just say they were clearly the result of a long, and hopefully fruitful, career as a sexter and he was clearing space for more. Again, to each their own, but in this case maybe a cramped domestic aircraft isn't the place to do this.

Sexting should always be as consensual as sex itself. Don't send unsolicited pics of your private parts to anyone unless you're sure they will appreciate them. Or be prepared to suffer the consequences. We all know about the former US Congressman with the unfortunate name of Anthony Weiner. He had a habit of sending photos of his, well, wiener, to people who didn't admire it as much as he did. It led to him being forced to resign from Congress in 2011 and, more recently, a repeat episode lead to the breakdown of his marriage. You should only send intimate pictures or texts to people you are in an intimate relationship with. Even then you should be wary. Relationships break down but a picture saved to a phone's hard drive can last forever.

Before you send a sext, make sure it's going to the right person. A name like David is pretty common and you might have several Davids stored into your phone's address book – make sure it's the right David. If you get it wrong then, frankly, you're in a sticky situation. The best thing to do in this instance would be to apologise fulsomely in a lighthearted way and explain it was intended for someone else.

SHOES WITHOUT SOCKS

Wearing shoes without socks is a fashion trend for men and women that seems to have lasted beyond a season. It's really a personal choice as to whether you like the look or not, but here's a word of advice: it's not great for your feet in the long run as they tend to perspire inside leather shoes, which don't breathe as easily as sports shoes, and all that foot perspiration is not good for your shoes either. If you want to pull off the no-socks look then invest in some secret socks. You can find them in the sock department of most department stores in a range of colours. Most people tend to go for the 'flesh'-coloured ones. The thing about secret socks, however, is they're often not 100 per cent secret depending on the design of your shoes and how low-cut they are. Loafers, for example, tend to expose more of the top of the foot than lace-up shoes. Flesh-coloured secret socks can take a cool look and make it look incredibly daggy if even a millimetre of sock can be seen, as I've yet to meet anyone whose flesh is actually the same colour as the socks. The best way to do it is to match your socks to your shoes as closely as possible, rather than to your flesh. That means black shoes with black secret socks – then, if a touch of your sock is showing it won't be so noticeable. When it comes to formal eveningwear for men, socks are as mandatory as a jacket and tie.

SINGLETS OR TANK TOPS

This item of clothing – or a T-shirt with no sleeves – is perfect for a day at the beach, or out walking on a hot summer's day. They should never be worn to a restaurant, unless it's a beachside cafe, or at a dinner table of an evening. This style of top is one that has different rules for men and women. A man who wore a tank top to the office would raise a few eyebrows and, depending on where he worked, might be sent home to change. A woman, however, can wear a sleeveless top or dress to the office and no one will bat an eyelid. Offices, however, are inhabited by men and women, and in the summer months many men are constrained by office dress codes into wearing more clothing than women in the office, which is why there is often a battle between men and women in the workplace about the temperature of the air conditioning. Women will probably disagree with what I am about to say, but my feeling is the men should have the deciding vote on this one – if you had to wear woollen trousers, a long-sleeved shirt and possibly a jacket and tie when it is forty degrees Celsius outside, you would also want the temperature in the office to be cool. If you're the kind of person who feels the cold but you also want to wear a sleeveless top to work – and why wouldn't you, when it's so hot outside – then consider leaving a cardigan or wrap in the office in case you get cold at your desk.

The same goes in winter. Theoretically the temperature in an office should be about the same all year round, but it often seems to be set at 'tropical' in the winter months and 'arctic' in the summer months. If everyone is wearing appropriate winter clothing in the cooler months then there should be no need for the temperature to be set so high. There is a famous photograph taken in the White House of Michelle Obama wearing a sleeveless dress shortly after her husband took office as President of the United States. There was outrage in the media at the time. How dare she expose her arms like that? It became known as Michelle Obama's 'right to bare arms'. But the photo was taken in February, and at that time of year it is freezing in Washington DC. There would have been snow on the ground, but Obama was dressed as if she were about to go to a summer garden party. I would put money on the fact that the heating was set to high and the men in the office that day were boiling. Dress appropriately and you can reduce your energy bills and help the planet at the same time.

SKYPING IN PUBLIC PLACES

Skyping or FaceTiming in public places requires headphones, and even then it can be irritating to the people around you. I travel a lot for my day job, which means

I often eat breakfast in hotel restaurants and spend a lot of time in airports. Technology allows us to keep in touch with people back home much more easily and cheaply than before. Skype and FaceTime are fantastic, but just because you can say goodnight to your kids via video call doesn't mean the rest of the airport lounge wants to hear it. Please put on headphones and try not to shout. If you have a bad internet connection, shouting into the microphone is about as useful as shaking your computer up and down to try to make them see you better. From my observations, most Skype calls in airports go something like this:

'Hi, can you see me? No? What about now, can you see me now? Hang on, I'll move to another seat. What about now, can you see me now? Well I can see you, you should be able to see me. What? Sorry, I can't hear you. I'm at the airport. THE AIRPORT. I'm boarding soon. SOON. Can you see me?'

And on it goes. When the connection is stable enough, the conversations, at least the ones that I've been privy to, can border on the mundane – unless you think a lengthy discussion of the minutiae of two people's days are worthy of a video call. The technology that allows for people to make video calls with each other and for virtually no cost is nothing short of amazing, and is exactly the kind of stuff we imagined would happen in the future when we were kids. The problem is that public wi-fi connections can be sketchy, especially if you're in a crowded place and hundreds of people are all trying to join the same network. If it isn't working and you need to shout to be heard then either go to a private place to make the call or resort to a voice call.

If you're concerned that people are eavesdropping on your conversation then let me assure you they are. That's what happens when someone in your immediate vicinity is talking in a loud voice – as an innocent bystander you can't help but be drawn in to the conversation. It's hard to tune it out, which means your conversation is dominating the entire room. I have no issue with people making phone calls – voice or video – in public as it seems to me that's the whole point of mobile phone technology. I just don't want to hear it. If you're in a crowded place like a bus or a train then try to keep your phone conversation short, and think about resorting to text or instant messaging if you want the contents of it to be private from the people around you. Certain conversations, such as what colour the baby's poo was today, are best had away from other people's ears (although I can't think why anyone needs to know that urgently unless it's suddenly lilac-coloured, then that would be cause for conversation).

SLANG

Slang is informal use of language and should be restricted to informal conversations and places. Slang words and expressions are also usually particular to a specific context or group, and when they are used away from that their meaning might not be fully understood or, worse, might be misunderstood. I used to have someone on my team at work who was a keen surfer and would sometimes refer to me as 'dude'. I would often get emails that began 'Hey dude,' and while I understood the lighthearted nature of his preferred way of addressing me, I often wondered if he was like that with people in the outside world and, if so, what they made of it.

Slang is best used verbally, as often a lot of the meaning can come down to the delivery. I received an email from a publicist recently that said she loved the latest edition of the magazine I edit and that the whole thing was 'on fleek'. Now, I could safely assume that was a good thing but I had to look it up to be sure. A quick Google search revealed that the expression has only been around since 2014 and is mostly used on social media. Basically it means polished and on point, and in this instance it might have been more appropriate if she had just said that. Sometimes words that might be perfectly acceptable for everyday speech with your cohorts are best left out of professional communications.

Try to avoid overusing the word 'like' as a conjunction to introduce reported speech unless you want to sound like a Kardashian. For example, in a professional setting, 'I was like, "no",' could just as easily be, 'I said no'.

The same goes with the use of jargon. Most jobs have their own set of jargon that everyone within that particular industry knows and understands, but you should be mindful of having conversations – virtual or real – with people in the outside world that are peppered with job-specific expressions. No one wants to get an email they have to translate via a Google search and, if they can't be bothered checking what something they don't understand means, then the entire point of your conversation might be lost. It can also make other people feel awkward or stupid if they have to ask what something means.

When it comes to professional communications, erring on the side of formality with written and spoken language will never get you into trouble.

SLURPING YOUR FOOD

Slurp . . . slurp . . . slurp. That's the sound I can hear coming from the table behind me as I sit in the Cathay Pacific lounge at Hong Kong International Airport waiting for my flight home. It's the sound of the person behind me slurping her wonton noodles in chicken broth. I had the same dish just minutes ago and found it to be delicious, and also very easy to eat without making that slurping sound.

Personally I find the sound disgusting and irritating – and for some reason it is done with such volume that it only serves to make it worse. Why is she

eating like that? Well, some people say it's for prac-
tical reasons – it lets air into the mouth to cool the
food as you eat it so as to avoid burning your mouth.
Who knew? So, should you do it? Well, technically it's
not an incorrect way to eat in the context mentioned
above, but that doesn't mean it's pleasant for other
people in the vicinity. People say 'When in Rome', but
I often think that's just an excuse for behaving inap-
propriately out of context. When it comes to eating
it's best to do what will cause the least discomfort to
others. If you were brought up with a cultural background where slurping food is okay then go ahead and
do it. If you do it out of context – in a country where
the custom is frowned upon – then be prepared to get
a few looks.

See also TABLE MANNERS.

SMOKING

Someone once asked me what I thought about the
etiquette of smoking. The etiquette of smoking? Is there
a correct way to give oneself lung cancer, I wondered?

But putting my personal prejudices about cigarette-
smoking aside, it is a habit that, while legal in various
situations, still causes offence and discomfort to some
people, so it is worth considering how to minimise
the impact it has on others. It's also something that
smokers, in my experience, feel strongly about, so
tread carefully if you want to take one on.

The person who asked me about the etiquette of smoking had a specific problem with cigarette smoke. He lives in an apartment building and the residents below him like to smoke out their window, and the second-hand smoke makes its way into his apartment. Yuck. As it happens I recently had a similar situation to deal with in my own apartment building. It was something that needed to be handled with caution, as issues in apartment buildings can easily descend into all-out war with body corporates and even police and lawyers becoming involved.

It was smoke of a different kind that was driving me crazy. My downstairs neighbours had a barbecue on their balcony, which they used nearly every night. The problem was that my bedroom was directly above their balcony and if the windows were open while they were cooking – and I wasn't home to quickly shut them – then my sleeping quarters smelled like cooked meat and smoke. I once lived above an Indian restaurant and even that didn't smell as bad. So I decided to confront the issue. I knocked on their door (breaking into a nervous sweat in the process) and calmly and politely asked if they would consider moving the barbecue to their other balcony at the rear of the building, off their kitchen. They seemed genuinely upset that the issue had caused me angst; they moved it immediately. I then left a bottle of wine at their door for their trouble. I was fortunate that there was a clear solution to the problem that wouldn't cause my neighbours too much trouble. Admittedly this is not always the case, but my point here is that a problem like this needs to be handled with tact and diplomacy.

Present your neighbours with a solution rather than just your problem. Is there perhaps another window they could smoke out of so it doesn't affect you so much? They clearly have an issue with smoke in their own apartment – hence doing it out the window – so chances are they will be able to empathise with you. Whatever you do, don't accuse them of anything. Say things like, 'You might not realise this, but . . .' and then go on to describe your problem. Or put yourself in their shoes and start with, 'I too like to smoke occasionally, but . . .' And if the problem ceases, then you should put a thank-you note in their letterbox or give them a small gift. Chances are they will be so touched by your appreciation that they won't forget about the issue in a week's time and light up again in the same window. Use the powers of your building's body corporate as a last resort – no one likes being dobbed on.

Smoking has become so marginalised in our society that one of the few places left where you can light up with impunity is in your own home. It is mostly banned in parks, beaches, sporting venues and on the doorsteps of public and some private buildings and there are moves afoot in New South Wales to have it (and barbecues) banned on apartment balconies. We could install smoking booths all over the city, such as the ones in some airports, and confine smokers to them like caged animals. Judging by how many people I've seen crammed into these booths no bigger than a garden shed when I've been transiting through an airport, the smokers don't seem to mind all that much.

As smoking is a legal practice, if someone isn't breaking the law, all you can really do to minimise the impact it has on you as a non-smoker is get out of their way. If they are breaking the law, then all power to you. If you're a smoker you should know the laws and obey them, not just because there are heavy fines for breaching them but also out of common courtesy to the people around you who don't smoke and don't want to smell like they do. And just because it's raining doesn't mean the four-metre law no longer applies.

See also E-CIGARETTES.

SNAPCHAT

Snapchat was founded by Evan Spiegel and Bobby Murphy while they were students at Stanford University, and its original name was, according to Wikipedia, Picaboo. The idea was for an app whereby users could share photos that were impermanent and disappeared once they had been viewed. You can probably guess from the original name and the temporary nature of the images that it was an app seemingly made for sharing images that people don't want to live on in perpetuity; that is, nude pics. Snapchat has changed a lot since it was launched in 2011 but the transient nature of the images shared on it hasn't. The only problem is, nothing shared online is completely impermanent. It is possible to take a screenshot of an image that has been shared on Snapchat while you're viewing it and save it to your camera roll. Snapchat's software will, most of the time, know that someone has done that and let the original snapper know – there are also apps, not endorsed by Snapchat, that are designed to make snaps permanent – but what's done is done, and if you've shared something that is potentially embarrassing then you are now relying on the good nature of the person who took the screenshot. If you'd rather not be in that position then just keep it fun and keep it clean.

Some people have yet to work out that most users view Snapchat with their phone in portrait orientation (that means holding the phone upright so the screen is larger in length than in width – holding it the other way, so it is wider than it is long, is called landscape orientation). Given that, it's best to shoot snaps in portrait mode, as having to turn your phone to landscape for the one person who hasn't worked this out yet quickly becomes annoying.

Snaps can be up to ten seconds long, but that doesn't mean you have to use all ten seconds. If you're just posting an image of your breakfast then maybe five seconds is enough. Snapchat is meant to be light and breezy; it's not for deep and meaningful contemplation. So if you post a ten-second snap of a stationary cafe latte then after about six seconds people will start to think, 'Why am I looking at this?' That's not the reaction you want. If you create a story, which is a series of snaps, then try to keep it under 90 seconds. If your story needs more than 90 seconds then maybe Snapchat is not the right forum. Also, don't post one-second snaps – what's the point?

If you're posting video snaps then think about the noise in the background. When people view it the sound will play automatically, and a loud music concert or a windy beach with someone screaming to be heard can be jarring. If you like to pass the time on public transport checking your various social media accounts, headphones are a good thing to use. Profanity is pretty common on Snapchat and not everyone around you wants to hear one of your friends yell out, 'Check out this beach, it's fuckin' awesome.'

Because Snapchat is not Twitter or Instagram, hashtags are really just for humour or to caption your photo, so there's no need for endless hashtags – you're never going to be trending.

Unlike Instagram, Snapchat is not about quality or perfectly composed images, but your post should be something worth sharing. Social media applications all kind of work in harmony – Snapchat is for things that are worth sharing but not good enough for Instagram and too trivial for Twitter. For better or worse, Snapchat lends itself to selfies, but a constant stream of selfies one after the other will start to feel repetitive. Mix it up a little.

Don't ramble. So many snaps are just people babbling in order to fill up their ten seconds. 'So here I am at the beach, it's a sunny day and it's really hot, I'm thinking I might go for a swim.' That kind of inanity is too common on Snapchat, and if ever there was a case where a single photo could say more than a ten-second video, this is it.

Send nude photos, even as private messages, with extreme caution. If you're sending a photo that you would never want anyone other than the intended recipient to view, and you would be mortified if anyone else ever did, then be careful. A quick screenshot now and a relationship breakdown or fight later and you could find your snap in places where you never intended it to be. And while you might be able to take legal action if this happens, the horse will have already bolted.

Don't Snapchat drunk.

Don't Snapchat while driving.

SPEAKING WITH YOUR MOUTH FULL

Never do it. While on the publicity trail for my first book, whenever I would do an interview I would invariably be asked what my number one pet hate about manners was. My number one bugbear when it comes to other people's behaviour, I would say, is lateness; however, that is followed very closely by someone speaking with their mouth full. As a general rule of thumb, when you have food in your mouth your mouth should remain closed until you have swallowed it. That means not putting more food or drink into your mouth and not attempting to speak. It is also generally accepted that you should chew with your mouth closed. It wasn't always the case that closed-mouth chewing was the rule, but thank heavens it became that way.

In her book *The Rituals of Dinner*, Margaret Visser explains that there were once regional variations in Europe as to whether the mouth should be closed or open while eating. Quoting a sixteenth-century French text, Visser says, 'Germans chew with their mouths closed, and find any other way of proceeding ugly. The French, on the contrary, half-open their mouths . . . The Italians are very soft in the way they eat; the French, who behave more robustly, find the Italian manner too delicate and precious.'

Over time in Europe and elsewhere it became the norm for people to eat with their mouths closed. Visser makes the point that the custom of closed-mouth eating is one of 'the most powerful and paradoxical injunctions of modern Western table manners'. Para-doxical because not only is it rude to chew like a wild animal in front of company, it's also rude to sit there in total silence. We are expected to make conversation at mealtimes. It is only when we have a very intimate rela-tionship with someone that we can sit and eat without speaking and not cause offence.

So, how do you speak and eat at the same time, you ask? The simple answer is that you don't. The trick is to talk between bites. Conversation while eating is a two-way street and you should take care not to elicit a response from a dinner companion while they have food in their mouth. Don't ask someone a question they cannot answer with a hand gesture just after they have placed food in their mouth.

If it happens that you are asked a direct question while you have a mouthful of food, the best course of action is to not answer until you have swallowed. Even if this takes a while, don't panic about the ensuing silence and try to speak. Eventually your fellow diner will get the message that your mouth can only do one thing at a time. You don't need to gesture at your mouth with a piece of cutlery, they'll get the message.

It's also a good idea to consume small bites of food. No one is going to take your plate away until you've finished, so what's the rush? Don't load up your fork too much. The French claim that eating slower, taking more time to chew, and taking smaller bites helps to keep one thin. It certainly makes it much easier to swallow quickly if you need to talk and provides you with less opportunity to make a pig of yourself: the more food you have in your mouth, the more chance there is of it falling out.

I'm not a huge fan of correcting people when they are doing something 'wrong', because we all do things incorrectly at times even if we try not to. If someone mispronounces my last name in a public setting – which is often – I let it slide most of the time because it only embarrasses the other person. It's the same when someone speaks with their mouth full. Correcting them only makes them feel bad and is a sure-fire way to ensure you're never invited to dine with them again. All you can do is grin and bear it, or try to avoid conversation until after the plates have been cleared.

SUICIDE

I had a friend who committed suicide last year and it was a very painful thing for everyone to deal with, not least because people rarely talk about suicide. Newspaper and television reports are extremely cautious about mentioning it as a cause of death. I found out that my friend had passed away on Facebook of all places. All of a sudden there were people expressing their grief and loss and I had no idea what had happened to her. It didn't take long to work it out, though. Personally, I think it's important that people know how someone died if only so they can have a better appreciation for what that person was going through at the time, but you don't need to go into great detail. You don't even need to say the word.

A few days after my friend passed away her parents posted a message on her Facebook account. It was a beautiful and heartfelt message that acknowledged that their daughter was in a 'dark place' and couldn't see the love and admiration people had for her. They provided some information about a memorial for their daughter and asked that people give a donation to Beyond Blue in her memory rather than send flowers. I guess years ago something like this would have been hidden and become the subject of gossip. Her parents were probably just using Facebook as a means to reach as many of their daughter's friends as possible without having to make dozens of calls, which, no doubt, would have been very upsetting for them. Their post was a reminder that social media is a form of communication between people and when a post is heartfelt and eloquent it can be an incredibly powerful thing.

See FACEBOOK for more about dealing with death on social media.

SUNGLASSES

There's a school of thought that suggests leaving your sunglasses on when you greet a person in the street is rude – like not taking your hat off indoors. I once conducted an interview with someone at an outdoor cafe and wore sunglasses. I was at the cafe before my interview subject and, considering it was a sunny day, I had sunglasses on. To be absolutely clear here, I wear photochromic lenses, the sort that go dark in UV light and then go clear when you're indoors. So really I was just wearing my normal glasses. Anyway, the interview went okay but I didn't feel a great rapport with the person I was interviewing, and later that day she sent my boss an email to say how rude I was. Naturally my boss brought it up with me and for the life of me I couldn't work out what I had done that was so offensive. My interview subject later told me it was because I didn't take my sunglasses off when I was talking to her. I had no idea it was such an issue for some people, but I guess not being able to see someone's eyes is disconcerting for the other person. So, there you have it.

In hindsight, it might have been better if I had asked the person I was interviewing if it was okay that I kept my sunglasses on as the sun was shining in my eyes. If you think asking permission is going a bit too far, then just make a passing apology in reference to why you're going to keep them on. 'I'm sorry about my sunglasses, but the sun is right in my eyes.'

SWEARING

Sometimes using a four letter word for emphasis is the best, most articulate way of expressing yourself. There is a huge difference between telling someone to 'go away' and telling them to 'fuck off', and there is really no other way of expressing the latter.

Shortly after my first book was published I received a telephone call from the office of June Dally-Watkins, the doyenne of Australian etiquette. Her assistant told me that she enjoyed my book and that she would like to meet me. When I met her she had a copy of my book with Post-it notes at certain pages and wanted to discuss some things with me. The first one was my use of a particular four letter word that begins with f and ends in uck. Needless to say, my, albeit minimal, use of profanity in my book didn't meet with her approval. I told her I was just trying to illustrate a point and I wanted my book to appeal to people who might have a more liberal view about the use of swearwords. To her credit she agreed that the world changes and language changes with it. I'm not sure she ever swears and I certainly didn't in her presence. When I was at school in the early 1980s, one of my teachers told me I wouldn't be going on to Year 11 if I didn't stop swearing. I thought he was reprimanding the wrong person, as all I had done was told another kid in the playground to 'shut up'. When I relayed the conversation to my mother later that night she informed me that in some households they consider that to be a swearword (whereas I grew up with four brothers, so someone was always being told to shut up).

Whether to swear or not is about using common sense and thinking about the appropriateness of the situation. If you're not sure if someone will be offended by the dropping of an f-bomb then perhaps find another, less colourful way of making your point. Or, test the waters with a softly spoken 'fuck' and see what reaction you get. If the other person recoils in horror, drop it from all further dialogue. If they smile, swear away.

In a professional setting it's always best to keep your language as clean and inoffensive as possible when you first meet someone. You'll soon work out how receptive they are to the occasional four-letter word. Swearing can also be used as a good icebreaker. I was hosting a conference in Melbourne a few years ago and one of the speakers used the word 'fuck' in the first few minutes of his speech when he lost his way in his presentation, and it got a good laugh from the room of five hundred people. That laugh probably also helped him overcome some of his nervousness. If you do it when you're giving a talk or presentation and it doesn't go down well, then drop it from the rest of your presentation.

Originality is also effective when you swear. Try to invent a new expression. It will have impact and people will remember it. I recently saw something as a comment on someone's Instagram that I can't repeat here, but let's just say it was a combination of four-letter words I've heard many times before but the syntax in this case gave them new meaning.

T

TABLE MANNERS

A lot of people are daunted by the complexity of table manners, but the truth is very few people will ever have the need to know how to use cutlery beyond a knife, fork and spoon. Eating dinner should be an enjoyable experience and not a stressful one. So here is my boiled-down version of what you really need to know about table manners. In a nutshell, behaving well at a dinner table is about making the experience of communal eating pleasant for your fellow diners. If you think about it, good table manners are based on making the crude business of eating and digestion more attractive. Stick to these rules and you can't go wrong.

The knife goes in your right hand. The fork in your left. Sometimes the fork can be used in the right hand if you're right-handed and you're eating pasta, which doesn't require a knife. When you set a table you should always set it for right-handed people, then it is up to a left-handed person to adjust the cutlery when the meal is served. Strict etiquette would say that left-handed people should use cutlery in the same way as right-hand people, but these rules were most likely laid down at a time when left-handedness was frowned upon in all parts of life, not just at the table. As a left-handed person, if it's more comfortable for you to eat with the fork in your right hand and the knife in your left then do so – it's far preferable than you struggling to do it the other way and, no pun intended, making a fist of it.

The spoon also goes in your right hand, and when you set a table you should place it (if it will be needed for the main course, or for a soup entree) to the right of the knife. If it's a dessert spoon then, to avoid confusion for the guest, you can place it across the top of the table setting, above the top of the knife and fork, or just bring the spoons to the table when the dessert is about to be served. A dessert spoon is usually more of an oval shape, a soup spoon is rounder, but these days most people and more casual restaurants tend to use one all-purpose spoon.

If there is a lot of cutlery in front of you then just start from the outside and work your way in. There will only be one set of cutlery per course. If you order something, such as crab, or certain kinds of fish, or oysters, that requires a specific utensil then don't be embarrassed to ask the waiter the best way to use it.

At the dinner table, nothing says ill-mannered more than holding cutlery like it's your first time. Knives and forks are not writing implements and should not be held as though they are. Nor should they be held in a closed fist like a tennis racquet. Hold the knife and fork by their handles and place your index finger along the top of each utensil. The tines of the fork and the sharp edge of the knife should be facing down and the handle of the utensil should be placed inside the palm of your hand – not poking through between the thumb and the index finger.

Use the fork to hold whatever it us you want to cut still and then cut it using a gentle sawing motion with the knife. Try to avoid clanking the cutlery against the plate at all times, and never allow the knife to screech against the plate when you've cut through your food. Now you're ready to put that delicious morsel into your mouth, and this is where things get tricky.

A fork can be used to scoop food such as peas to your mouth with the tines of the fork facing upwards, but it should be done with the right hand (which means putting down your knife and swapping hands). The reason for changing hands is that if you're right-handed and you try to do it with your left hand you risk spilling them with your wobbling hand. If you're left-handed then do it with your left hand if you want to.

To eat soup, dip the spoon into the soup away from your body then sip the liquid, without slurping, from the side of the spoon. Don't insert the entire bowl of the spoon into your mouth. The theory behind dipping the spoon away from you is that scooping it towards you is more likely to slosh soup into your lap. It is perfectly fine to tilt the bowl slightly – again, away from the body – to get the last spoonful or two of soup, but it is not okay to bring the bowl to your mouth.

Don't speak with your mouth full.

Eat quietly. Do not slurp, smack your lips, crunch or make other noises as you chew or swallow. This should be easy if you keep your mouth closed when you're chewing and swallowing. Some foods, such as potato chips and crispy bacon, will always make a noise as you crunch them, and while that is perfectly acceptable there should not be a competition at the table to see who can make the most noise.

Don't lick your fingers.

Don't lean back on the legs of a dining chair.

Don't smoke at the table even if all your dining companions are smokers – even some smokers find the combination of smoke and food disgusting. Always go outside to smoke.

If it's a formal dinner, don't take your pre-dinner drink with you to the table.

A napkin is essentially there to protect one's clothes from spillage. When setting a table, it should be folded square and flat and laid on each place setting, over the charger plate (a large plate that is used as an under plate for formal dinners – food is not served on them, the food plate for each course is placed on top of the charger) if there is one. Folding napkins into swans or Sydney Opera Houses is best reserved for children's parties. Unfold your napkin – don't snap it open with a flourish – and place it in your lap. In a restaurant you don't wait for the waiter to do this for you. Personally I would rather do it myself than have someone fussing around in my groin area. Don't blow your nose with a napkin either. If you get up to leave the table at any time, including at the end of the meal, place your napkin on the table to your left. Don't screw it into a ball or refold it – just place it. You can also leave it on your seat.

On last thing about napkins: it's not a serviette, unless you happen to be dining in France. Anywhere else the word just sounds pretentious and the generally accepted terminology is napkin or table napkin. If you ask for a serviette in the United States, people will look at you as if you've asked for a giraffe.

Elbows on the table are not the end of civilisation. Actually eating with your elbows on the table, however, is close to it. There are some situations, especially in noisy restaurants, where elbows on the table might be necessary as you lean forward in order to be heard, but remove them when you are taking a bite to eat.

Keys, handbags and mobile phones don't belong on the table. If you must have your phone on the table then place it face-down. In a restaurant your handbag should go on the floor or on a hook under the table if there is one (some restaurants will actually provide a small stool for a handbag to keep it off the floor).

Wait until everyone at the table has the meal in front of them before you start to eat.

If the meal involves shared dishes then serve others before you serve yourself. If it's a big table with a lot of people then take the dish, serve those next to you and yourself then pass it along. If you don't know the person next to you and you don't feel entirely comfortable serving them, then you can always ask, 'Would you like me to serve you some?' Most people will be relieved they don't have to do it themselves and make a mess of it. If it's a big and heavy dish, hold it for someone and let them serve themselves and so on.

Look someone in the eye when you clink glasses, not at the glasses, and actually make contact with the glasses, don't just wave them in the air.

If a toast is to be made it should be from one of the hosts, unless the host asks another guest to do it beforehand. There's no need to respond to the toast, except with a 'Cheers' and possibly also a 'Thank you for having us' or some such thing if the toast was made by the host.

Red wine is served in balloon-shaped glasses and white wine in glasses with a narrower opening. Red wine needs to breathe and the wider glass creates a greater surface area for it to do so. For that reason wine – red or white – should only ever be poured to the widest point in the glass, and not as close to the brim as possible.

Sometimes water can also be served in a wineglass, but is often served in a short whisky-style glass.

When pouring wine, don't hit the glass with the top of the bottle and try not to let the wine 'chug' as you pour. When you're pouring you should turn the bottle as you lift it back from the glass to avoid dripping wine on the tablecloth.

When you've finished eating, place the knife and fork beside each other on the dinner plate in the twelve and six o'clock position with the handles extended slightly over the lower edge of the plate. If you need to leave the table – you know, to make that telephone call that you would never make at the table – and you haven't finished your meal, there is a way to let the waiter know. If it's soup, leave the spoon in the ten and four o'clock position. If you are done with the soup, leave it in the twelve and six o'clock position. To show that you are still going with a main course you leave the knife and fork on the plate with the fork in the two and eight o'clock position and the knife in the ten and four o'clock position. The same goes for dessert.

There are a few occasions when abandoning cutlery altogether and eating with your hands is perfectly acceptable:

Corn: Corn on the cob is a pain to eat with cutlery and can be picked up and held at each end, either in the hands or with special corn handles.

Olives: Olives are always eaten with your fingers. Dispose of the pits from your mouth into the palm of your hand and place them on your plate. If you're serving olives as a hors d'oeuvre then provide a dish for the pits.

Fruit: Some fruits, such as cherries and plums, are also always eaten with the fingers, as are strawberries if they still have the hulls on them. Remove cherry pits or grape seeds from your mouth in the same manner as for olives.

Bacon: Crispy breakfast bacon, if it's too brittle to spear with a fork, can also be picked up to eat.

Chops: Picking up chops or chicken legs in your hands and gnawing at them was a wartime food-saving measure. Some posh caterers have decided they make good finger food, but it's impossible to eat these without making a mess of your hands (and sometimes your shirtsleeves).

Chips or fries: If they are a side dish they may be picked up with your fingers, but if they are on the same plate as the main course you should eat them with a fork.

Pizza: Pizza can be eaten either with your hands or with a knife and fork. But don't pick bits off the pizza and eat them as if the crust is a snack plate.

Mangoes: To prepare a mango, hold it upright and cut as big a slice as possible down each side, avoiding the stone. Place the slices flesh-side up and score a checkerboard pattern into it, then turn the skin side from convex to concave. You can then easily remove the mango flesh with a knife or spoon, or, if there are no implements at hand, you can use your teeth to remove each chunk.

Bread: Your bread plate is to your left. You eat bread with your hands by tearing off bite-sized pieces – don't cut it with a knife. If you are sharing a butter dish, take some butter off the dish and put it on your side plate with the bread – don't spread directly from the butter dish.

You don't need to make orgasmic sounds to let people know you are enjoying your meal. A simple 'This is delicious,' or 'This is the best roast chicken I've ever tasted' will suffice.

Don't push your plate away from you when you've finished, or announce 'I'm done.'

Don't leave the table until the host does, or without asking to be excused.

If you want to fill up your wineglass, top up everyone else's glass first.

See also CHAMPAGNE, CHOPSTICKS, FOOD ALLERGIES, SLURPING YOUR FOOD, SPEAKING WITH YOUR MOUTH FULL.

TALKING IN A RESTAURANT OR CAFE

Talking is fine – that's one of the reasons people go to restaurants, to catch up with friends. But yelling is not the same thing. Remember that you're in a public place and not only can other people hear what you're saying, they'd probably rather not be hearing it. If you're in a noisy restaurant then lean in to speak to your dinner companion – don't yell for them to hear you. As I write this section I am in a cafe that is not particularly noisy. There is a man at the next table who is yelling at his companion to the point where everyone in the cafe knows that he has a new girlfriend and that she's awesome. He's even yelling with food in his mouth, which frankly takes great skill. My problem with both of his actions – yelling and speaking with his mouth full – is that he has no regard for the people in his immediate vicinity.

Be considerate about the people around you. And if you want to chat with someone over the phone while you have your morning coffee on your own and you have to speak loudly in order to be heard, then maybe speak to them later in a more appropriate place or text them instead. It doesn't always work – I once asked the woman at the next table to me who was dining and chatting on the phone if she could keep her voice down a little, and she covered her phone and said that she was having an important conversation with someone. Trust me, she wasn't, unless you think a conversation about whether she and her husband should go skiing in Aspen or Japan this year is important enough to annoy everyone within earshot. I was extremely polite and apologetic when I asked her to pipe down and she was also polite, but snippy, when she informed me after she ended the conversation that if she was having her conversation in person then I would have had to hear both sides of it and it would have made twice as much noise. Well, she had a point, but I could hear both sides of the conversation as it was, and she possibly wouldn't have had to yell at the person opposite her, unless they were hard of hearing. She left the restaurant and probably thought I was a local crazy person. You can't win 'em all, but you can try.

TAXIS

I live in Sydney and our city's taxis are nothing short of disgusting. To rework a joke by Woody Allen in the film *Annie Hall* – they're so bad and there are not enough of them. The introduction of ride-sharing services like Uber into the Australian market has meant that taxis have lifted their game, but only slightly. For the benefit of readers who have not experienced a Sydney taxi first-hand, let me summarise: the cars are usually filthy, the drivers rarely know how to get where you want to go and they are in large part terrible drivers with little regard for anyone else using the roads. Which brings me to why taxis are a manners issue. Their navigation skills and the odour of the car you can do little about, but you can help your taxi driver to be a better road user. For example, when you want to get out, don't let the taxi stop in the middle of the street – make them pull over and stop somewhere appropriate.

When it comes to taxi passengers you can lead by example. Don't leave a mess in the taxi, and tip your driver if they do a good job. Rewarding good behaviour reinforces further good behaviour. Have your cash or credit card ready before you get to your destination so you can get out as quickly as possible and avoid holding up traffic. And don't steal someone else's taxi. We all know what you're doing when you walk outside a building and see a bunch of people waiting for a taxi and then walk down the street a few metres to try to grab the next cab before it gets to the queue. You're not being clever, you're being a selfish arsehole.

TELEPHONE GREETINGS

Caller ID has more or less eliminated the need to say who it is when someone answers your call, and has also altered the way we answer a call. If I know it's John calling by the caller ID on my phone then I will most likely say 'Hi John' when I answer it, and then we begin our conversation. That's fine between friends, but in a business setting there is no harm in being a little more professional when answering the phone and making calls. If someone answers your call with just a 'Hello' or by announcing their name and/or business then you should respond with something along the lines of, 'Hello, this is David Meagher from [company]. I'm calling to speak to [person].' If you're returning someone's call and the phone is answered by a receptionist or personal assistant rather than the person you're calling, then you should say you're returning the particular person's call. That lets them know that you don't need to be vetted or given the third degree about who you are and where you are from and what the call is concerning. You should speak clearly and slowly so the person has a chance to catch your name. When answering your own phone and you don't know who is calling – or even if you do – then say your name rather than just 'Hello'. I usually just say 'David speaking', but will also sometimes say my full name. Personally I hate telephone greetings that are a mouthful, such as 'Good morning, this is David from Such and Such, how may I direct your call?' Such speeches are often said so fast as to render them mean-ingless. If your company has guidelines on how you should answer the phone and wants you to deliver a monologue when you do it, then slow down and say the words clearly and with conviction.

TEXTING

These days emails can seem like formal communication. A written letter – that is, one on a piece of paper – is so rare that it is shocking to receive one. I'd like to be the kind of person who sends handwritten notes to people but my handwriting is so hard to read there would be no point. I'm obsessed (see OBSESSED) with beautiful stationery and would love to send hard copy letters rather than emails, but our printer at home ran out of ink so long ago that I'm not even sure they make ink cartridges to fit it anymore. Texting has, whether we like it or not, become one of the most common forms of written communication between people.

In my 2005 book on manners I wrote, 'Before you go ahead and send someone a text message it's a good idea to make sure they know how to accept one.' How quaint. If there are still people out there who don't know how to send or receive a text message then I haven't met them. I also wrote in my previous book that 'Text message should be viewed as a very informal means of communication and used accordingly.' It is informal but, at the same time, its use is commonplace.

Can you send your boss a text to say you're sick and won't be in today? Yes.

Can you terminate an employee via text? Strictly speaking, yes, but you still shouldn't.

Can you end a relationship with a boyfriend or girlfriend via text? Yes, but you will be spoken about unfavourably by that person for your cowardice.

Can you send a text as an invitation to dinner? Yes please.

Can you send a text as a thank-you? Well, it's better than no thank-you at all.

Can you send a text as a condolence message? At least it lets someone know you're thinking of them, and it's quite possible they're not in the mood for talking.

The truth is – and I think I speak for many people here – most of the time I'd much prefer to receive a text message than a telephone call.

How you compose your texts is entirely up to you, but you should think about the person who is going to be receiving it. When I send a text for business I make sure I spell words correctly, use proper punctuation and capital letters, and I never use abbreviations such as LOL or OMG (well, almost never). If you do use abbreviations like those, make sure you know what they actually stand for and don't use so many of them that it requires someone to google what they mean in order to understand your text.

If you know someone is travelling or is in a different time zone to you, then think about the timing of your text if it isn't urgent. An email might be better in this situation so their phone doesn't *bing* and wake them up.

If you text someone for the first time then say who you are just in case they don't have your number stored in their phone.

See also EMAILS DURING MEETINGS.

TEXTING WHILE DRIVING

See ROAD RULES, but in a nutshell, never do it.

THANK-YOU NOTES

Etiquette guides of yesteryear would discuss at great length when a thank-you should be sent and what form it should take – as in, should it be handwritten or could a telephone call suffice. These days, if you get a thank-you at all you're extremely grateful. Strictly speaking the form of the thank-you should follow the form of the invitation. If you received a written invitation – that is, on actual paper – then you need to send a handwritten thank-you back.

If you go to someone's house for dinner, or they take you to a restaurant and pay, or if they host a social gathering at their house, you need to say thank you in some way. You should also send a thank-you note if someone gives you a gift. There are no rules on what form the note should take, but if it's a particularly thoughtful gift then a handwritten note is a nice touch.

Buying a box of blank cards, such as the ones you find at art galleries, makes it a much easier thing to keep on top of. You don't have to make a special trip to a newsagent and you'll have some on hand when you need a birthday card for someone in a hurry. You can also send a handwritten thank-you on stationery.

If the invitation came by email, or by phone call or text message, then a thank-you can be sent in the same mode, but a phone call is always nicer. People who've hosted a large party, however, are usually exhausted the next day and so sending a thank-you text or email is perfectly acceptable. These days handwritten thank-you notes seem to be extremely rare – except maybe in appreciation of a wedding or baby gifts – which makes them all the more valuable when you get one. Sending a card to someone if you've been a guest in their house, or if they've gone to a lot of trouble in hosting a party, tends to stick in the mind of the recipient. When sending a written thank-you, make reference to the particular event or gift.

When you send it is also important, but not crucial. Unlike dating there's no three-day rule here. Call or text the day after to say thank you and you can debrief about the night's goings-on. Calling two or three days after is also fine. Just don't leave it too long. But, a late thank-you is better than no thank-you at all. Someone once told me about a well-known fashion designer who sends his thank-you notes as he is leaving an event. That sounds just a little too soon and robotic.

TIPPING

In most countries tipping is a reward for good service. In certain places such as the United States, wages for restaurant, bar and hotel staff are low, and workers rely on tips to supplement their wages. The by-product of low wages is, usually, that the cost of your meal has been kept lower, so a good tip in the US is not out of the question. Tipping in the US is more or less expected, and if you've ever tried to get out of a taxi or leave a restaurant without tipping you may have experienced exactly how expected it is. When you travel, it's a good idea to research what the tipping culture is in the country you're visiting. Always ask someone you trust – hotel staff will tell you if you need to tip taxi drivers or restaurant staff or not.

Technologies such as contactless and online payments have significantly reduced the tips that some people earn. If you settle your restaurant bill with

EFTPOS then either leave a tip in cash on the table or in the tip jar, or use the function on the payment machine for tipping. Home-delivered takeaway food can be easily ordered online these days, with payment made by credit card. If there's no facility for adding a tip to the bill at the time of transaction then give your delivery person a cash tip if they have, for example, delivered promptly or delivered in bad weather, or climbed six flights of stairs to get to your apartment. Tipping in this situation is not just about a job well done – it's also about ensuring you get a similar level of service the next time you order. Delivery people and waiters always remember the good tippers (and the lousy ones).

In hotels I tip when I arrive (to the porter who carried my bags and sometimes to the doorman who got them out of the taxi) and I tip again when I leave, as a thank-you. How much you tip is up to you, but notes are preferable to coins. In some cities, like New York, some doormen expect you to tip every time they open the door for you or hail you a cab, which is why the country has never bothered to get rid of its one dollar bills. It can be excessive and downright annoying, which is why I tip well when I arrive and leave it at that. Tip the housekeeping staff each day if they have done a good job making up your room.

You should tip your hairdresser or barber at Christmas time, especially if it's the sort of salon where it can be hard to get a booking. If your hairdresser goes out of the way to squeeze you in at the last moment, you should tip them in appreciation of the effort they have gone to.

Tip your housekeeper or cleaner at Christmas time.

Tip a removalist if they have done a good and speedy job and didn't break anything. Tip a furniture delivery person too, or just offer them a drink.

If you use valet parking then tip the person who takes your car when you drop it off – don't forget, they will be driving it and you want them to make sure it is not scratched getting in and out of a parking spot.

Tips don't have to be huge but it's important to remember why you are tipping someone. It's either because they have done a great job and are not on a huge income, or because they have done something that you would rather not do, like clean your house or lift heavy furniture or suitcases.

Strictly speaking, tips are not necessary in Australian restaurants. Staff working in restaurants are covered by an award and are paid well compared to similar jobs in some other countries. Casual workers are also paid loadings for working on weekends and public holidays. However, that doesn't mean you shouldn't tip if you have had an exceptional meal or extraordinary service. As a general rule, ten per cent is an acceptable amount to tip in Australian restaurants. You don't need to be excessive about it, it's just a gesture of thanks.

TOILETS

'Which way should the toilet roll hang?' I had no idea this was an issue but people tell me it is. The answer is simple: the roll hangs with the paper rolling over the top of the roll and down the outside. Hanging it the other way (with the paper rolling down the inside) makes no sense and just looks like you've made a mistake. If you have children or pets who are fond of unravelling an entire roll of toilet paper just for fun then consider storing it out of reach – for example, on top of the toilet cistern if possible. In my experience it's the rolling aspect of the toilet roll holder that appeals to children and animals. Speaking of toilet paper, if you are having people over for dinner you should add checking that there is enough toilet paper in the bathroom to your list of things to do before the guests arrive.

'Should the seat be left up or down?' In my first book on manners I devoted a large chunk of words to this subject, as people kept telling me that was what they wanted other people to know. It's a vexed issue, apparently. I don't want to spend too much time going over old ground, so, for the sake of keeping the largest number of people happy, the seat goes down when the toilet is not in use, and so does the lid. If you're a man and you live alone or with other men, and only men ever visit your home, then you can leave the lid and the seat up. If, however, you live in a mixed house and the issue

is causing a lot of friction between men and women then, for the sake of everyone's sanity – because, let's face it, discussing what position the toilet seat should be in is hardly one of life's great questions – consider either gender-split bathrooms or getting one of those amazing Japanese toilets that can be programmed to automatically raise the seat and/or lid when you approach, and lower them back down when you're done. Or just get used to leaving the seat in the down position.

Public toilets: A public toilet is not a free zone where you can do away with all the basic civility you have acquired in your life. I am speaking here of men's public toilets. I have no idea what women's toilets are like, but my female friends tell me it is nothing like the way I have described the men's toilets to them. I work in an otherwise civilised office, but the men's toilets often look like Jackson Pollock and Christo have been in there collaborating on an art installation. If you don't know what I mean by that then just know this: it's a mess that even barely toilet-trained children wouldn't make. Just behave and remember that other people have to use it, and someone also has to clean it.

Talking to people: Personally I think the workplace toilet is a conversation-free zone, mostly because when I go in there it is not just to relieve myself but also to have a few minutes of peace and quiet away from the office. Female friends tell me that women like to chat in the bathroom. My experience is that men mostly don't. I won't go into the psychology of why that is except to say that you should respect someone's desire to have a talk-free toilet session. You can usually tell by someone's body language whether or not they are up for a chat while they wash their hands at the basin or stand at the urinal – head down and avoiding eye contact is a sure sign chitchat is off the menu. And please, don't mistake the raised eyebrows and briefest of hellos (g'day, how're you going, et cetera) for an invitation to talk. I'm just acknowledging that I know you, that's all.

Talking on the phone: I take my phone into the bathroom with me at work because – well, it's none of your business why. I just do. Sometimes I look at Instagram or Twitter – like I said before, a bathroom break is a respite from the business of my job. I never talk on the phone in a public bathroom as they are usually like echo chambers and everyone else in the room would hear you. I also switch my phone to silent when I go in there so if it does ring no one will hear it, and if I type a message to someone you won't hear the *click-click-click* of my typing, which for some reason in a bathroom (which is all hard surfaces) sounds like someone doing a tap dance. A lot of people, however, do seem to have an issue with people talking on the phone while they sit on the toilet. My question is this: why does it matter where someone is calling from (unless it's a video call)? Even if you know by the echo or the sound of running water that the person on the other end of the line is sitting on a toilet, does it really make a difference to the conversation? I mean, it's not like you can smell through the phone and, not wanting to put too fine a point on it, you possibly have their undivided attention when they are on the toilet as there is not a lot else to distract them. There's no hygiene issue here – germs cannot be spread over the phone and, in most cases, people don't share their mobile phones with other people. If, however, you're aware there is a queue of people waiting for a toilet cubicle then make your call elsewhere – it's not a phone booth. I remember as a child going on holidays and seeing a telephone next to the toilet in a hotel room and thinking that was the height of luxury and sophistication. I also thought it seemed important and official – the person who answers the phone must be very busy if they can't have a few minutes to themselves. People have been talking on phones on the toilet ever since the invention of the telephone; mobile phones have just made it easier. But, keeping in mind that some people find it distasteful, it's best not to tell people where you are – if they ask if you're in the toilet because of the echo, just say you live in a minimalist house – and don't flush until you've hung up. There's no explaining your way out of that one.

If there's a queue of people waiting to use the toilet, then you should make it snappy. When it comes to public toilets men are the lucky ones – we are usually provided with urinals, meaning the bathrooms can accommodate more people more quickly. Women often have to queue up for a toilet cubicle. If there is a queue then normal queue etiquette applies: don't push in, don't get unnecessarily impatient and do let more needy people go ahead of you if you can. When it's your turn, don't waste time doing things that could just as easily be done elsewhere, such as reapplying makeup, brushing your hair or texting/talking on the phone.

TRAVELLING ON AN AEROPLANE

Elsewhere in this book I have addressed specific issues about plane travel, such as the use of overhead lockers and reclining your seat. What follows here are my golden rules that will make travelling on a plane that much more bearable for everyone.

Everyone has a horror travel story and they almost always involve people rather than mechanical failure. No matter what end of the plane you travel in, at some point in the journey you're going to come face to face with other people and, as we know all too well, other people can be hell.

When travelling long distances became common-place for most people, after World War II, existing etiquette books were revised to deal with the issues and a whole lot of new guides sprang up. How to deal with strangers on public conveyances was one of the most worrisome things for many people. Travelling meant mixing with people that one didn't know, almost a new concept for the time.

In 1953, Valerie Winton wrote in her book *Etiquette for All Occasions* that travel shouldn't be treated differently to any other aspect of modern life. 'We cannot allow our manners to become casual just because travelling is such an everyday affair,' she wrote. Hoorah to that.

In order to assert one's social standing, a great deal of attention in old etiquette books was devoted to what to wear while travelling. These days almost anything goes in terms of apparel on a plane; and, while it is certainly a myth that being dressed up will get you an upgrade, being poorly dressed definitely won't advance your cause. Several airlines have a policy of not upgrading passengers if they are poorly dressed regardless of what their frequent flyer status with the airline is. For some airlines that means a shirt with a collar and a jacket for a man, and no jeans or trainers for anyone. That doesn't mean that other people in the first class cabin won't be shabbily dressed, but they may have paid full price for their tickets, which means they didn't have to pass scrutiny at check-in.

Just as minor disturbances, like someone kicking the seat behind you, can turn your trip into a nightmare, so too can minor courtesies turn it into something less tiresome and vaguely bearable.

Don't push and shove in the security screening queue. Everyone knows by now that you need to take out your laptop and that there are restrictions on liquids, so make the necessary preparations while you're waiting in line, not when you get to the front. Don't argue with the security people – they didn't make the rules and they are just doing their jobs. If you need to repack your bag and put your shoes back on after screening, then take your things and move away from the conveyor belt to do it so that other people's bags can come off.

If it's a long security queue and you see a parent travelling with small, tired and potentially troublesome children, let them go to the front of the line. Children and slow-moving queues are a lethal mix.

Don't hog the arm rest. In economy class there's at least one armrest per passenger, so don't take more than your allocation. If you're sitting three across then be mindful of the person in the middle. The person on the window side has an armrest and the side of the aircraft to lean against; the person on the aisle has the aisle-side arm rest and easy access to get in and out of their seat. The middle position, on the other hand, is the pits. Everyone has their preferred seats when they travel and I don't think I have ever heard anyone say 'I really love sitting in the middle, squashed between two people.' Cut them some slack and let them have both armrests if you can.

Don't hog the toilet, either. Why you would want to spend more time in there than is absolutely necessary is beyond me, but do try to leave it in a fit state for the next person.

If you don't want to speak to the person seated next to you, be nice about it. Pick up a book, put headphones on (you don't have to actually play music) or just be honest. Make very brief chitchat and then say, 'It was lovely talking, enjoy the flight.'

If you use headphones to listen to music on the flight then make sure the volume isn't so loud that the person next to you can also hear your music.

There is a class structure on planes – but that doesn't mean that flight attendants are servants. Don't treat them as such.

Don't fart in your seat. The cabin pressure does things to your body that, believe it or not, causes more flatulence than normal. Just because no one can hear you let off over the roar of the engines doesn't mean you should. It's also worth noting that newer aircraft like the Airbus A380 and the Boeing 787 Dreamliner are much quieter than older aeroplanes and, guess what, we *can* hear you!

Don't try to cram a month's worth of luggage into the overhead compartment, or rearrange or squash someone else's luggage to fit yours in.

Don't wear too much perfume and don't wear too little deodorant. Don't brush your hair while you're sitting in your seat unless you're sure you can do it without getting hair all over the person next to you.

Don't get excessively drunk – you'll feel like crap when you land, and if you're abusive to airline staff or passengers you might feel even worse if you are removed from the plane by police officers.

Do stop your child from kicking the seat in front of them. Don't ignore your child if they are screaming their head off or running around annoying other passengers.

Don't rest your head on someone's shoulder if you don't know them.

If you have a window seat you should try to go to the bathroom when the person next to you goes, so you don't have to wake them up or crawl over them to get out. If you have a weak bladder, you should request an aisle seat when you make your booking – leaving it until check-in might be too late.

The air vent above your head is for you. It's not for the person next to you, and if they want cold air blowing on them they can open their own vent.

Eating a meal on a plane, in economy class at least, requires you to cut your food with your arms held close to your body to avoid elbowing the person next to you. Yes, it's an unnatural way to eat your meal, but so is flying in a giant metal tube.

Don't use the entertainment handset to scratch your groin *inside* your trousers. I've seen it happen.

Do travel with sanitary wipes. I do, and I wipe down the tray table, arm rests and entertainment handset after I've taken my seat. I've been on enough planes and seen enough bad behaviour (see the example above) to know how filthy a plane seat can be. Planes are turned around in airports far too quickly to be cleaned properly, in my opinion (have you ever looked down the crack between the seat and the side of the plane? It's like a food museum down there), and I'd rather people look at me a little oddly than catch something.

See also AEROPLANE TOILETS, BAGGAGE CAR-OUSELS, BOARDING AN AEROPLANE, CHILDREN ON AEROPLANES, IN-FLIGHT ENTERTAIN-MENT, OVERHEAD LOCKERS ON AEROPLANES, WINDOW SHADES ON AEROPLANES.

TWITTER

I'm on Twitter – you can find me at twitter.com/davidfmeagher – but I wouldn't say I engage with it in any meaningful way. For me Twitter is more of a news resource than a vehicle for expressing my thoughts about whatever is happening in the world or what I have had for lunch/will have for dinner/am planning to watch on television, et cetera. If you're on Twitter then I'm sure you know the kind of people I am referring to here. There are people I follow on Twitter who tweet several times an hour every day. Frankly, I don't know how they do it and hold down a job at the same time. Who knows, maybe they don't have jobs? Maybe tweeting like this *is* their job? Or maybe they're doing it to build up their Twitter followers and their professional profile.

Frequency of tweeting is a big issue. It's a different equation to other social media apps like Instagram, which is image-based rather than character-based. As

I mentioned above, three Instagram posts per day is a good limit. If you posted every hour on Instagram you would very quickly start to lose followers, but Twitter is different. Twitter is fleeting. Depending on how many people you follow, a tweet can be buried under hundreds of other tweets in a matter of minutes, so you can tweet more often. I once heard a social media expert say that if something was worth tweeting once then it is worth tweeting five times. You can tweet something repeatedly at different times of day, on different days, if you think it's something your followers really want to know. This usually refers to tweeting links to stories rather than a 140-character musing on your latest bowel movement. You can use the acronym 'ICYMI', which stands for 'in case you missed it', to let people know you've tweeted it before. ICYMI is also good for drawing your followers' attention to a link to a story online that might have been published some time ago but you have only just discovered it.

Twitter has a place for everyone and if you are one of those people who likes to tweet their every thought throughout the day then, yes, you will lose followers. But at the same time you will find followers – probably people who also like to tweet ad infinitum – who will stick with you. One of the things about Twitter is it gives a voice to people whose only need is to have a voice – they don't need someone to answer back, they just need to be heard. In fact, they just need to think they are being heard.

Twitter only allows posts of 140 characters so it lends itself to all manner of tricky abbreviations to pack as much into a tweet as possible. Try not to make every word an abbreviated one. If you look at your tweet just before you post it and it doesn't contain a single vowel then perhaps rethink how you've worded it before sending. A 140-character long message is a simple thing to digest if expressed properly; it shouldn't feel like cracking a secret code.

Don't overshare. Don't post about your bowel movements or inanity like 'urgh, train delayed.' If you're posting because you want to let other people know there are delays on a particular train line then give them relevant information, such as which line and how long the delay is. Sharing things on Twitter just for the sake of it can become habit-forming – the more you do it, the more you're inclined to do it. Maybe it's just me, but I tend to unfollow those people. After you've composed your tweet and before you hit the 'tweet' button, read over it and ask yourself, 'Is this really worth sharing with the world?'

If your feed is just a whole lot of links to your website or blog it will look like shameless self-promotion. Vary it a little with a few links to other sites or retweets interspersed with 'Check out my new blog post'.

Hashtags can add a little humour or help with further explanation. They are also a great way to connect with other people tweeting about the same subject and to build followers. But a tweet that is just hashtags and nothing else makes it look like you think in hashtags, and that's a silly way to think.

Do you need to follow someone back if they follow you? Not necessarily. If it's a close friend or a colleague then not following them back might appear like a snub. If it's someone you don't know then there is no obligation. At the same time, you shouldn't expect people to follow you back just because you followed them. They will probably take a look at the sort of things you tweet in order to make a decision about whether to follow you or not. If you follow a celebrity or a company then don't expect them to follow you back. Bill Gates (twitter.com/billgates), for example, has more than 30 million followers, but at the time of publishing he was following 169 people, so there's a good chance that if you follow him he won't follow you back.

More than any other social network, Twitter seems to be the place where people are most likely to express their opinion about something. Think about what you are going to tweet before you send it. If it's a controversial opinion, or you're buying into a controversial argument that is happening online and in the wider world, then think about whether or not you are adding anything to the discussion. If you're ever in doubt as to whether or not what you want to tweet might cause offence then sit on it for a while before you hit the tweet button. A cooling-off period is helpful when tweeting or acquiring a new puppy – they are both decisions that can come back to haunt you if you're not careful. Hot-headed tweets can fire up a Twitter war with other users and it can be very hard to extract yourself from it and recover.

Don't hate-tweet celebrities or well-known people unless it's your goal to get on Jimmy Kimmel's Mean Tweets segments. If that is your goal, maybe get another one. While it might be tempting to let a politician know how you feel about something, remember that potential employers will look at your Twitter feed when doing a background check on you. That doesn't mean you should censor yourself, it just means to think before you tweet.

Don't drink and tweet.

Don't drive and tweet.

See also 'LIKING' (ON FACEBOOK, INSTAGRAM AND TWITTER).

U

UNFRIENDING SOMEONE

Social media has in many ways redefined the concept of friendship. I'm sure I speak for many people when I say that I have a lot of friends on Facebook, Instagram and Twitter that I rarely – if ever – see in real life (I use the term 'unfriending' here, but it also applies to unfollowing people on social networks such as Twitter, Snapchat and Instagram). Being friends on Facebook doesn't necessarily imply the same level of affection as being friends in the real world. So if you no longer want to follow someone on Facebook because you don't like the types of posts they share, or they post too frequently, then the way to do that is to unfollow them. It's very easy, it usually doesn't cause any offence and it's a much nicer word than 'unfriend'.

If you want to stop seeing a particular person's posts in your timeline then all you have to do is find a recent post by them and click on the arrow in the top right-hand corner of the post to view the drop-down menu. There you'll see an option to 'unfollow' the person and, as it says, you will stop seeing posts but stay friends. If you really want nothing more to do with them then go to their profile page and choose 'unfriend' from the 'Friends' menu. This is something you should reserve for people you really don't want to be friends with in any capacity. We all have those people in our lives; friends of friends who you, for one reason or another, don't particularly like. Or people you've had a huge falling out with and want nothing more to do with. It's nice to be liked by everyone, but as you get older you realise how unrealistic that is. If you don't want to be friends with someone in the real world then don't accept their Facebook friend request if you get one.

A word of warning about unfollowing someone: if it's someone you see socially from time to time and you are no longer receiving their posts on Facebook, chances are you might miss an important moment in their life. It might be a holiday, the death of a parent, or a rant they went on about something or other. They might ask you if you've seen it and if you don't know what they are talking about then the cat is well and truly out of the bag. Feigning ignorance and claiming that you haven't been on Facebook for ages won't work if you have indeed been on Facebook, because the person you have unfollowed will quite possibly have seen your activity. Depending on how you have your privacy settings configured, something as innocent as liking someone else's post could be your undoing. So, if you unfollow people on Facebook then get your privacy settings figured out. Or blame it on that annoying Facebook algorithm, but if you do that you should know what you're talking about.

USING SIR OR MADAM

It sounds terribly old-fashioned, but I do use 'sir' and 'madam' to address people on occasion – mostly if the person is a complete stranger and I don't know their name, and only if they are an adult. I do so because it's disarming. If you accidentally bump into someone in the street and apologise by saying, 'I'm so sorry, madam,' most women will be shocked someone could be so formal in their manner that they won't chastise you for not watching where you were going. If you need to ask directions of a man in the street, opening the conversation with 'Excuse me, sir, can you tell me . . .' makes it quite unlikely you'll be told to piss off.

Strictly speaking, the correct way to address a letter to someone whose name you don't know is 'Dear Sir or Madam'. You can also use 'To whom it may concern' if you'd rather be completely gender neutral.

V

VAPING

See E-CIGARETTES.

VEGETARIANISM AND VEGANISM

I didn't include this in the food allergies section as choosing not to eat meat or animal products is usually more of an ethical choice than a medical one. I'm neither of these two things but I respect people who are. I like animals and choose to live with one, and I would be mortified if anything were to happen to him in the way of animal cruelty, but I have no problem with eating other animals. I am inherently aware of the fundamental contradiction in that point of view.

I never get worked up about some moron who hunts lions or elephants in Africa for fun because I am part of a system that kills animals every day for food and clothing and other items. As a magazine editor I'm occasionally asked if I have a problem with featuring fur in the fashion pages of the magazine and I have to say that I don't, as we feature leather and other animal products, and I fail to see what the difference is. This is one of the reasons I respect people who make the choice not to kill animals for food – they are people who have courage in their convictions.

Therefore, if I invite someone to my house for dinner and they are a vegan, I make sure I prepare something they can eat. That doesn't mean that you have to prepare a special meal for that person. You can make everyone go meat-free for the evening – the trick is not to tell anyone. There's no need to explain that because so-and-so is coming to dinner we are all going to go without meat this evening. Just do it and don't make a big deal out of it. I've done it many times and no one even mentioned it. Yotam Ottolenghi has some delicious vegetarian dishes that make great dinner party fare because they are quite labour intensive, so still have a substantial wow factor when presented at the table.

Vegan desserts are a challenge unless you only want to serve fruit. However, Nigella Lawson has a recipe for a vegan chocolate cake in her book *Simply Nigella* that is quite easy to make and delicious to eat.

If you are a vegan or a vegetarian then it's good to let people know when you accept an invitation to dinner so they can prepare their menu accordingly. Telling your host when you walk in the door puts them in an awkward situation – it's not a restaurant, it's someone's home, and you might end up eating nothing but potatoes and salad for dinner.

VOICEMAIL

Not long ago I was at a lunch with a group of people and one of them looked at her phone to see she had a missed call and a new voicemail message. On discovering this she announced to everyone that she thought leaving a voicemail message for someone was the height of rudeness. Others in the group were surprised by her reaction, but I knew exactly where she was coming from.

Let me explain by way of example. I have a friend who almost never answers his mobile phone. He also almost never calls me back, either. You might be asking why we are friends, but that is not the issue here. His not responding to my missed calls infuriates me, so when I do finally get to speak to him I can't help but ask why he didn't call me back. 'You didn't leave a message,' he will say, very matter of fact. 'The missed call *was* the message,' I'll respond. 'It said, I called, call me back.' 'Just leave a message and if it's urgent I will call you straight back,' is his response.

In my first book on manners I devoted several pages to the right way to leave a voicemail message for someone: what to say, how to say it, and how to use voicemail to make your busy life easier. Now I can categorically say that I never listen to voicemail messages, which is why I also rarely leave them. Once upon a time we didn't have a missed call function on our phones, we just had answering machines, so you had to leave messages, otherwise no one would know that you called. Today I am a strong believer that the missed call is the message. If it's urgent then I'll send the person a text, which requires much less effort to read than dialling your voicemail, listening to it, hanging up and then calling me back. If I'm just calling to say hello then I send a text message saying so immediately after the missed call so the person knows it's not urgent and to call me back whenever they are free.

In a work situation if I call someone on their landline and their voicemail kicks in, I hang up and either call back later or send the person an email. If you are trying to get in touch with someone urgently out of office hours then send them a brief text. Many people try to not look at their emails out of hours so they might not get an emailed message in time. Explain as best you can what the urgency is in your text so they can be prepared when they call you back.

Back to my friend who thinks voicemail is the height of rudeness. She said she much prefers a text message to a voicemail, which led one of the people in the group to declare that her parents don't know how to text so she has to listen to their voicemails in case it's urgent. My friend's response: 'I just call my mother back when I can, and if I get six missed calls from her in a short space of time then I know it's urgent.' While there is a strong element of truth to this, if you do get a voicemail message you should make an effort to listen to it and respond to it as promptly as possible.

If you do leave a voicemail message then do the receiver a favour and speak slowly and clearly, especially if it's someone you don't know and you are leaving your telephone number. Slow down and repeat your number, especially if you have a private number and it wouldn't have displayed with the missed call message. Don't make the receiver of your voicemail message listen to it three times to decipher it, especially if you actually want them to call you back (and if there is no need for the person to call you back, then say so when you begin your message). You should also leave more than just your name and phone number. In the briefest way possible, tell the person why you are calling them – at least that way they can have whatever information they need on hand when they return your call. If I get a message from someone I don't know and they don't say what it's about, then I don't call back.

W

WALKING AND TALKING

There is a person in my office who seems incapable of sitting still while he talks on the phone. Most of his calls seem to come to his mobile phone so as soon as he answers he's up and pacing about the area. He's also quite a loud talker, so it's annoying and distracting for everyone in his immediate vicinity. The rest of us, for the most part, all follow the rules of open-plan office life and take our calls at our desks, and make an effort to keep our voices down. If you want to make a private call then you either go to a dedicated area or go outside. The problem is, large companies today love mobile phones because they reduce the need for employees to have a dedicated desk and landline. Reduced need for people to be in the office means fewer desks, fewer desks means smaller offices and lower rent. The concept used to be called 'hot-desking' but now it's called an 'activity-based workplace' (or sometimes even 'hotelling', in an attempt to make it sound more appealing), and the proliferation of mobile computing and phones has made it a lot easier for people to be freed from the shackles of their desks.

Back to my annoying colleague – it turns out there might be a scientific explanation for why he is incapable of sitting still and talking. An August 2016 story by Tom Popomaronis on *Inc.com* looked at research that had studied how the brain works when you talk to someone. 'Over time, as you talk face-to-face with people, your brain connects elements such as vocal tone, word choice, emotion, and gesture all together,' he says. 'When you talk on the phone, the physical feedback you'd normally get isn't available. The connections you've formed, however, mean that the parts of the brain associated with movement still fire.' Which is why some people just can't sit still when they talk on the phone.

Knowing that it's natural for people to want to move around when they're on the phone, and considering that movement has been associated with higher creativity, businesses might do well to rethink their sit-in-your-seat approach to calls. For instance, executives could ensure that individual offices are oriented so as not to inhibit movement, or they could hold non-video conference calls in larger areas so that the person who has the floor has a choice about whether to be physically engaged.

Similarly, individuals who work in call centres might benefit from having sit–stand or standing stations.

If you are faced with a distracting pacer of your own, my advice is that if you can't beat them, join them. Start pacing.

Just kidding. Pacing while on the phone at work is a perfectly normal reaction to the absence of a stimulus you normally get during conversation. Still, if you're distracted by someone doing it, politely let them know you're having trouble and offer an alternative, such as a work-appropriate fidget toy, to strike a compromise.

WALKING AND TEXTING

Some years ago I received a press release from a university trumpeting the results of a recent study into sleep problems. The results of this extensive survey concluded that people who sleep with their dogs – wait for it – sleep less deeply than people who don't, and as a result complain about being tired during the day. No shit, Sherlock. As the owner of a dog that some-times sneaks onto my bed after I have fallen asleep I, and probably every other dog owner on the planet, could have saved these researchers a great deal of time. Sometimes things are just so obvious they don't need an expert to explain them – they just are.

A report published in 2014 by the University of Queensland about a study into the effects of walking while texting came to the conclusion that texting and, to a lesser extent, reading on your mobile phone while you walk 'affects your ability to walk and balance,' the authors said. 'This may impact the safety of people who text and walk at the same time.' Stop the presses! Who knew that if your eyes are not on where you are going then you run the risk of falling over or walking into a light pole or oncoming traffic?

I shouldn't get worked up about this but I can't help it. I'm sick of having to walk down the street and having to dodge people as they walk, faces down, looking at their smartphones. Or trying to walk down a flight of stairs while some idiot in front of me is reading on their phone and walking slowly enough that they don't fall over, and therefore slowly enough to annoy the person behind them. What annoys me about this is that the person who is walking and looking at their phone just assumes that you will get out of their way. Sometimes, when I'm really annoyed by it, I like to accidentally-on-purpose bump into the person and then apologise profusely. I figure that if more people do that then they might get the message that it's a pain in the neck to walk and text.

I really don't mind if someone wants to walk into the traffic or cross a pedestrian crossing with their eyes attached to their screen rather than the oncoming cars – really, that's your choice and if you want to get hit by a car then go for it, but try to be mindful of the pedestrians behind you and in front of you as you do it. Really, is what you're reading so important that you have to do it right now, while you're walking? I've looked over the shoulders of some offenders and from what I've seen it really isn't, unless you think scrolling through Instagram is so vital at that point in time that you just can't leave it until later. If it is that important – if you really need to send that text now – then consider standing to the side of the stairs or footpath and stopping for a moment to send your message. Then start walking again, and walk with purpose.

Our maybe our cities should start designating lanes on sidewalks for texters in the same way that we have cycle lanes and split lanes for people walking in opposite directions. It's not as mad as it sounds. *The Wall Street Journal* reported in September 2014 that the Chinese city of Chongqing unveiled a lane for people who want to walk as they use their mobile phones. 'Cellphones; walk in this lane at your own risk' is printed in the lane in white lettering. The adjoining lane reads 'No cellphones'. Then there's the town of Augsburg in southern Germany that, in early 2016, installed traffic signals in the ground at two tram crossings to prevent people from walking into oncoming trams while looking down at their phones, after a teenage girl died after walking in front of a tram while looking at her phone and listening to music on her headphones.

WHAT?

Don't say 'What?', say 'I beg your pardon.' My parents would say that to us when we were kids, to the point that it was just one of their sayings. At the time we weren't exactly sure why we should avoid saying 'what?' when we didn't hear something clearly; we just knew we shouldn't. Of course, as we got older we realised that it was short and rude.

WHO IS COMING TO DINNER?

When you receive an invitation to dinner or to a party, is it okay to ask who else is coming? If it's a large party then it's okay to ask. A good host shouldn't leave their guests in the dark too much either; it's good to tell people just a sample of who else is going to be there as it can make the invitee feel more comfortable about going to the party, especially if they don't know many of your friends. Giving your guests the heads-up about who is attending means they don't have to spend time guessing or asking around – that only leads to disappointment when uninvited people realise they didn't make the cut.

However, saying yes to a dinner invitation and immediately asking who else is going makes it sound like your attendance is conditional on the guest list. It's entirely conceivable that your friend has friends that you don't particularly care for, but after a while most people know this, so they either don't invite people who don't get along or make an effort to ensure they are not seated near each other. You should always accept an invitation to dinner in good faith – faith that the other people there will be fun and interesting, and faith that your host will not invite any of your sworn enemies.

If it happens that you've had a huge falling out with someone and you're sure the person inviting you to dinner wouldn't know about it yet, then it's probably a good idea to mention it. You don't need to go into all the gory details. You can just say something like, 'Dinner sounds wonderful and I would love to come, and I don't want to be a pain, but I should probably tell you that I've had a bit of a falling out with X, so maybe it's a good idea if we're not at the same table for a little while. If you've already invited X that's fine, I'll sit this one out, but thank you for inviting me.' No real harm can come from something like that, and if your response to the invitation ever gets back to the person you've had a fight with then you're in the clear as you have behaved admirably and with consideration to the other person's feelings.

Closer to the date, it's acceptable to ask who will also be there, as this demonstrates enthusiasm for the coming event rather than implying that your attendance is conditional on the company.

WINDOW SHADES ON AEROPLANES

Sometimes when I'm on a plane I wish I had a selfie stick even though I have no interest in taking selfies. I could use it to reach the window next to the seat in front of me and push its window shade down. I realise some people can sleep in blinding light and can even do that on a plane, but leaving the window shade up is annoying to your fellow passengers who have the unusual need for darkness to fall asleep. Read the room – or the cabin, in this case. If everyone else is trying to sleep or watch a movie but your window shade is up, then perhaps consider lowering it and using the reading light.

If someone near you has their window shade up while you're trying to get to sleep or watch a movie then it's perfectly acceptable to ask them politely if they wouldn't mind lowering it. I've done this on numerous occasions and often find out the person next to the window didn't realise the rest of the cabin was in darkness.

WORKPLACE ATTIRE

How someone behaves is one thing, how they dress is quite another. First impressions really do count and before anyone has heard you speak or shaken your hand the first thing they will notice about you is what you look like. A big part of that is what you are wearing.

Whether your employer has a formal or casual dress code, you should put some effort into what you wear to the office. You don't have to spend a lot of money to look good – just make sure your clothes fit properly and are appropriate for your position. If a tie is optional then opt to wear one as often as possible. If you think a dress or skirt might be too short for the office it probably is. Don't carry your bits and pieces around in a nylon backpack – quality accessories last for years and can make an average-quality, affordable outfit look a million dollars. T-shirts are for weekends, and thongs for the beach.

You should put together a working wardrobe. For a man the goal should be to eventually have five good-quality, well-fitted suits. Then you need five shirts, a few ties and a few pairs of shoes, and that's it. Take a leaf out of Barack Obama's book – the fewer decisions about clothing you have to make, the more you can focus on the big decisions to be made. In a profile in *Vanity Fair* in 2012, the president told writer Michael Lewis that he only wears blue and grey suits so that he can pare down decisions. 'I don't want to make decisions about what I'm eating or wearing. Because I have too many other decisions to make,' he said. Most of us are not running a country, but that doesn't mean we couldn't benefit from some time-saving in the morning.

If you have a more casual workplace then put together enough suitable clothes that can be mixed up to last you for five days without having to do laundry or dry-cleaning. Having a working wardrobe serves two functions. First, you don't have to think too hard before you get dressed in the morning, which makes getting out of the house that much quicker. And, second, having clothes that you only wear to work helps to clearly delineate between work time and when you're on your own time, just by what you are wearing.

Learn to care for your clothes properly. Hang up jackets and pants on their proper hangers as soon as you take them off. Dry-clean sparingly – it's not great on your clothes, and most of the time just a light steam will do the trick. You can buy a clothing steamer from most electrical and department stores and they will significantly cut down on the amount of money you spend on dry-cleaning, and extend the life of your garments. Woollen knitwear doesn't need to be dry-cleaned either. You can hand- or machine-wash them with an appropriate detergent, but be careful if the label says 'dry clean only', as you will have no recourse if you damage it. Having said that, I have never damaged a knit item by washing it.

Store your ties properly. I like to roll mine up and put them in a drawer – it helps get the creases out – but hanging them is fine too.

If you don't know how to tie a tie or iron your shirt or polish your shoes, go to YouTube, where you will find plenty of instructional videos to guide you.

If you buy good-quality leather shoes then you should store them with shoetrees in them.

Business shirts are best laundered at home and line-dried. Sending them out to be washed and ironed shrinks them and shortens their life span. If you want to minimise ironing then take your shirts out of the machine before the spin dry and hang them up on hangers on the clothes line.

See also ACTIVE WEAR, PALE SUITS, SHOES WITHOUT SOCKS, SINGLETS OR TANK TOPS.

X

X-CULTURAL SENSITIVITIES

It's never a very good idea to begin a sentence with the words, 'I don't mean to sound racist but . . .' or 'I'm not a racist, but . . .' Similarly, I hate it when someone begins a conversation by saying, 'Don't take this the wrong way'. If there is a wrong way something might be taken, then find a better way to say it – or don't say it at all.

If you find yourself in a situation such as a casual conversation or a workplace meeting where someone is being offensive about someone else's race, gender or sexual preference then you should stand up for that person if they are either not part of the conversation or not willing to speak up. Sometimes people won't speak up if someone is being racist, sexist or homophobic – even if it is directed at them – because they don't want an argument, don't want to draw attention to themselves or have simply heard it all before. You can speak up on their behalf, however, without embarrassing them. You don't need to say, 'I find what you just said about Mary offensive.' You can just say, 'I find what you just said offensive.' You don't have to be the target of an offensive comment to be offended by it.

You've probably seen those videos on YouTube of people being abused by a stranger on public transport because of their race or skin colour and wondered what you would do if you were a bystander in that situation. A situation like that can easily turn violent, so you should weigh up the likelihood of that happening before you intervene. If the abusive person is drunk then direct your attention to the victim rather than the abuser. If you're sitting next to the person who is being abused, try to engage them in a conversation. Generally speaking, bullies are after a reaction and if they don't get one they will move on to something else, so engaging the person who is on the receiving end of abuse will focus their attention on you and not the abuser.

If you want to engage with the person making the abusive comments then try not to embarrass the person who was the target of abuse; speak to the offender more generally about their behaviour and ask them to be quiet. Abusive behaviour can lead to criminal charges so making a video recording with your phone will go a long way towards helping someone if they want to press charges. When the abuse stops or the person moves on, make sure the person who was the target is okay, and offer to make a witness statement to the police if they want to go down that path (you should also give the person your contact details in case they want to make a police statement at a later date and need witnesses). They may just want to forget about the incident, and you should respect someone's choice not to pursue legal recourse.

Different cultures have different standards of behaviour and dress, and you should respect those when travelling. If you're travelling to a Muslim country you may be expected to wear more modest clothing than you would normally. If you're travelling to a destination you haven't been to before and you're unsure about the standards of dress then do some internet research before you pack.

Y

YELLING

Is very rarely necessary. In a place where people value peace and quiet, such as in a restaurant or cafe, or in an office, a museum or even a shopping mall, if you feel the urge to yell then maybe get closer to the person you are trying to communicate with or wait until you are both in a place where you can speak at normal and sensible volume. Yelling should be reserved for emergencies or to warn people – You know, for expressions such as 'Watch out!', where speaking normally would be pointless.

YOUR FLY IS OPEN

It happens. Sometimes you leave the house and you have forgotten to zip up your fly. I've done it enough times for me to almost develop a compulsion about it – I am always checking that my fly is done up. People – people with zipped up flies, that is – seem to think it's embarrassing to point out to someone that their fly is half-mast and they are at risk of exposing themselves to the world. It's far more embarrassing, however, to be the person with the undone fly. Go on, help a fellow human being out and politely let them know. 'Politely' means taking them aside or gesturing to them surreptitiously. You don't need to shout it across the office floor. If there's no way of letting a friend know without potentially embarrassing them then send them a text message. There isn't, but there should be an emoji for it.

YUM CHA

See DIM SUM OR YUM CHA.

Z

ZEBRA CROSSINGS

I know – no one calls them zebra crossings anymore, except perhaps people who watch old episodes of *Sesame Street*. That said, I needed an entry to file under Z and this one works.

There are two ways to navigate a pedestrian crossing – to use the more common terminology – as a pedestrian and as a driver, and most of us are both of these things.

As a pedestrian you should not charge out onto a pedestrian crossing without waiting for the traffic to stop first. That's just common sense, but it never ceases to surprise me how many people assume that cars, buses and semitrailers will just magically stop for them when their feet, or the wheels of their pram, touch the white stripes. Maybe they will when we're all passengers in driverless cars, but that's a little way off. When you're sailing a small boat on the harbour, the rule is that smaller craft give way to bigger craft, presumably because the larger craft can do significant damage to the smaller craft. It's worth bearing this in mind even though the laws are different when it comes to the roads. A driver is always in the wrong when they hit a pedestrian but, even though I've never been hit by a car, I'll wager that it's little comfort once you've been hit to know that you were in the right, no matter how minor your injuries. So wait for the traffic to stop before you step out.

There is a pedestrian crossing two doors down from my house, and it's outside a day care centre. The number of times I have seen parents push their prams out into the crossing without any regard for the oncoming traffic is scary. It's just some painted lines on the road, and offers about as much in the way of protection. You still need to think about not putting yourself in harm's way.

You should also acknowledge a driver when they stop – a small wave, a smile, or even a raised eyebrow will do the trick. By doing so you're not only thanking them for stopping, you're also reinforcing their behaviour. When you're having a crappy day and the traffic is bad and other drivers cut you off or don't let you in, having a pedestrian wave thanks at a crossing can make all the difference.

Some months ago I was walking through Sydney with a colleague who was visiting from New York. As we crossed the road at a pedestrian crossing I gave a small wave to the driver who stopped for us. My friend then said to me, 'You know a lot of people, don't you?' Confused, I asked why she thought that. 'You waved at that driver, and the other one at the previous crossing. I explained to her that's what Australians do. It's not really a wave, it's just a sign of recognition that the driver stopped for me. She though this habit was very quaint and said if she did that in NY people would think she was mad.

Maybe so, and if that is a concern of yours and if you're not going to wave then the least you could do is to not dawdle on the crossing – make it snappy. We all have places to be.

As a driver, don't be a dickhead and blow your horn at people to hurry up. And if someone waves at you then wave back. It's just good manners and it won't kill you.

ACKNOWLEDGEMENTS

I hate lateness in myself and other people more than anything else. To me showing up late is a sign of disrespect towards the person you're meeting with. I'm perpetually early for things and although it sometimes annoys people I make no apology for it. Sometimes, however, you just can't avoid being late. Whether it's bad traffic, or being held up at work, or a dog that just won't do his business as speedily as you would like him to, there are often personal issues that conspire to make you late for something. I was late delivering this book to my publisher, Meredith Curnow, at Penguin Random House Australia, and when I say late I mean really late. I would like to take this opportunity to formally apologise to Meredith and to thank her for her eternal patience with my repeated requests for deadline extensions, and then for persevering when that revised deadline came and went. I promise it won't happen again. A huge thank-you to my editor, Kathryn Knight, for whipping my manuscript into shape and for her invaluable suggestions that have enhanced this guide to modern manners.

I would also like to thank my partner, Lane Finlayson, for his forbearance. Our days off work don't always coincide and often when they have I have spent them writing. I'd also like to acknowledge his contribution to this book in various ways, but specifically for reminding me to hit 'command-S' on the keyboard every now and then.

I would also like to thank Rodney Hanratty, John Lam-Po-Tang, Phillipa McGuinness, Helen Trinca, Stephen Brook, Susan Kurosawa, Jonathan Lobban, Fiona McCarthy, Ken Thompson and Sandy Bresic for their advice, encouragement, support and professional wisdom, as well as offering up the occasional story of bad (and good) manners.

Some small sections of this book have previously appeared in *The Australian* newspaper, and some reference has also been made to my 2005 book, *It's Not Etiquette: A guide to modern manners*, published by Random House.

NOTES

EMAILS
Nikki Gemmell, 'Email sign-offs say a lot about the sender', 27 June 2015, *The Australian*, www.theaustralian.com.au/life/weekend-australian-magazine/email-signoffs-say-a-lot-about-the-sender/news-story/eea0cc1c133ec03b4d839c4271a689b3

FORMAL WEAR
Descriptions for this section have, in part, been taken from: John Morgan, *Debrett's New Guide to Etiquette and Modern Manners: The indispensable handbook*, Headline, London, 1996, p. 336

INTRODUCTIONS
Noreen Routledge, *Etiquette for Australians*, Dymock's Book Arcade, Sydney, 1944, p. 63

MOVIES

The Sunday Times, 'Lovers lose to cinema texting', 21 October 2013, *The Australian*, www.theaustralian.com.au/news/world/lovers-lose-to-cinema-texting/story-fnb64oi6-1226743483064

OPEN-PLAN OFFICES

Maria Konnikova, 'The open-office trap', 7 January 2014, *The New Yorker*, www.newyorker.com/business/currency/the-open-office-trap

Lindsey Kaufman, 'Google got it wrong: The open-office trend is destroying the workplace', 30 December 2014, *The Washington Post*, www.washingtonpost.com/posteverything/wp/2014/12/30/google-got-it-wrong-the-open-office-trend-is-destroying-the-workplace/

PARTIES AT HOME

Courtney Rubin, 'Queen Elizabeth's party planner is proud to wear $35 shoes', 23 April 2016, *The New York Times*, www.nytimes.com/2016/04/24/style/queen-party-planner-lady-elizabeth-anson.html

SPEAKING WITH YOUR MOUTH FULL

Margaret Visser, *The Rituals of Dinner: The origins, evolution, eccentricities and meaning of table manners*, Grove Weidenfeld, New York, 1991, p. 309

TRAVELLING ON AN AEROPLANE

Valerie Winton, *Etiquette for all Occasions*, World Wide Mail Order Pty Ltd, Sydney, 1953, p. 37

WALKING AND TALKING

Tom Popomaronis, 'You know those people who pace while on the phone? Science say they have it right, after all', 23 August 2016, *Inc.com*, www.inc.com/tom-popomaronis/you-know-those-people-who-pace-while-on-the-phone-science-says-they-have-it-righ.html

WALKING AND TEXTING

Ma Si, 'Chinese city launches special lane for cellphone addicts', 15 September 2014, *The Wall Street Journal*, blogs.wsj.com/chinarealtime/2014/09/15/chinese-city-launches-special-lane-for-cellphone-addicts/

WORKPLACE ATTIRE

Michael Lewis, 'Obama's way', 11 September 2012, *Vanity Fair*, www.vanityfair.com/news/2012/10/michael-lewis-profile-barack-obama/

ABOUT THE AUTHOR

David Meagher is the editor of the monthly luxury lifestyle magazine *WISH*, inserted into *The Australian* newspaper. He has written for *The Sydney Morning Herald*'s Domain and Spectrum sections, and has been a senior writer and fashion editor on *The Australian Financial Review Magazine*. His books include *Fashion Speak* and *It's Not Etiquette: A guide to modern manners*.